New York Apartments

New York Apartments

Editor:
Paco Asensio

Editorial coordination and text:
Ana Cristina G. Cañizares

English copyediting:
Juliet King

German translation:
Haike Falkenberg / Inken Wolthaus

French translation:
Michel Ficerai

Art direction:
Mireia Casanovas Soley

Graphic design/Layout:
Pilar Cano

Photo editing:
Marta Casado

Published in the US and Canada by
teNeues Publishing Company
16 West 22nd Street, New York, N.Y. 10010, USA
Tel.: 001-212-627-9090, Fax: 001-212-627-9511

Published in Germany, Austria and Switzerland by
teNeues Verlag GmbH + Co KG
Am Selder 37, 47906 Kempen, Germany
Tel.: +49-(0)2152-916-0, Fax: +49-(0)2152-916-111

Published in UK and Ireland by
teNeues Publishing UK Ltd.
77 The London Fruit & Wool Exchange,
Brushfield Street, London El 6EP, UK
Tel.: +44-(0)20-7655-0999, Fax: +44-(0)20-7655-0888

www.teneues.com

Editorial project:

Domènec 9, 2-2
08012 Barcelona. Spain
Tel.: +34 93 218 30 99
Fax: +34 93 237 00 60

e-mail: loft@loftpublications.com
www.loftpublications.com

Printed by:
Gràfiques Ibèria, S.A.
Barcelona, Spain

September 2001

Die Deutsche Bibliothek - CIP-Einheitsaufnahme
Ein Titeldatensatz für diese Publikation ist bei der Deutschen Bibliothek erhältlich.

Life in New York is many things, but not serene and restful. The city is notorious for its towering skyscrapers that echo the noise of the streets into a roar of muffled voices, honking cars, and stagnant pollution. Yet despite the chaos, New York City mesmerizes people from around the world with its charisma. This urban kaleidoscope continues to woo visitors and to retain the loyalty of its residents.

NEW YORK APARTMENTS offers a glimpse of some of the city's homes, namely those created and designed by the country's most sought out architects and designers. The reader will enjoy the variety of stunning apartments that range from minimalist to postmodern and that include the typical New York loft, additions to houses, and functional flats. Every apartment has a well thought out style and distribution that adapts to its owner's needs and lifestyle. Due to the nature of the surrounding landscape, the spaces are molded to the city's characteristics and make the most of the unique urban panorama while providing a quiet refuge in the midst of this hectic concrete jungle.

Das Leben in New York ist alles andere als Gemütsruhe und Erholung. Die Stadt ist für ihre himmelsstürmenden Wolkenkratzer berühmt-berüchtigt, die den Lärm und das Chaos von den Straßen zurückwerfen und zu einem bunten Getöse gedämpfter Stimmen, hupender Autos und stockender Abgase machen. Trotz alledem lassen sich die Menschen nach wie vor vom Charisma der Stadt hypnotisieren, und das urbane Kaleidoskop hüllt weiterhin Besucher wie loyale Bewohner ein.

NEW YORK APARTMENTS bietet Einblick in die privaten Domizile der New Yorker, insbesondere in solche, die von den ausgesuchtesten Architekten und Designern des Landes geschaffen und gestaltet wurden. Der Leser kann sich durch die überwältigenden Wohnungen blättern, vom Minimalismus bis zur Postmoderne, in Form von Anbauten an bestehende Häuser, typischen New Yorker Lofts oder funktionellen Apartments. Jeder einzelne Entwurf hat seinen eigenen Stil und eine individuelle Raumaufteilung - sorgfältig durchdacht, um sich den Bedürfnissen und dem Lebensstil des Besitzers anzupassen. Der Charakter der Umgebung beeinflusst die Gestaltung der Räume, die den Eigenarten der Stadt entgegentreten, indem sie das Beste aus dem einzigartigen urbanen Panorama machen sowie eine stille Oase des Rückzugs inmitten dem hektischen Betondschungel bilden.

La vie à New-York est tout sauf calme et sereine. La cité est célèbre pour ses imposants gratte-ciel qui semblent se renvoyer les uns aux autres, comme un écho, le bruit et le chaos de la rue, en un rugissement tumultueux de voix étouffées, de klaxons et de pollution stagnante. Pour autant, tous demeurent comme hypnotisés par le charisme de cette ville, kaléidoscope urbain continuant d'accueillir tant ses visiteurs comme ses occupants fidèles.

NEW YORK APARTMENTS propose une vision fugitive des foyers de ses habitants, plus précisément ceux créés et conçus par les architectes et designers les plus recherchés du pays. Le lecteur pourra vagabonder entre ces demeures captivantes, du minimalisme au post-modernisme, prenant la forme d'extensions de maisons, de loft new-yorkais typique ou d'appartements fonctionnels. Chacune a acquis ses propres style et distribution de l'espace, pensés avec soin pour s'adapter aux nécessités et au style de vie du propriétaire. Étant donnée la nature du paysage environnant, les espaces épousent les caractéristiques de la ville, révélant le meilleur d'un panorama urbain unique en son genre, et offrant par ailleurs un refuge tranquille au cœur d'une trépidante jungle de béton.

New York Apartments

Manhattan Apartment with a Terrace

Shelton, Mindel & Associates

Photos: © Michael Moran
Completion date: 1998

The construction of this apartment was designed to integrate the project and the city. Other objectives were to take advantage of the four facades and the roof, and to create an ap-propriate setting for a collection of furnishings and artwork by 20th century artists and architects. The lower level divides the public and private spaces with several sitting areas. One of them takes the form of a circle inside a glass box with a double spiral stainless steel staircase leading to the roof. The top level houses a more intimate living area that also serves as an exhibition space. The project features an interesting division of space and the use of materials like aluminum, structural white glass, and cherry wood.

Mit dem Bau dieses Apartments sollten Projekt und Stadt integriert werden. Außerdem wollte man die vier Fassaden sowie das Dach nutzen und einen angemessenen Ort für die Möbel- und Kunstsammlungen von Künstlern und Architekten des 20. Jahrhunderts einrichten. Auf der unteren Ebene werden öffentliche und private Räume durch verschiedene Sitzgruppen getrennt. Eine ist kreisförmig und liegt innerhalb eines gläsernen Würfels mit einer doppelt gewendelten Treppe aus Edelstahl, die auf das Dach führt. Im obersten Geschoss befindet sich ein gemütlicher Wohn- und Ausstellungsraum. Interessant bei diesem Entwurf ist die Raumaufteilung sowie der Einsatz von Materialien wie Aluminium, weißem Glas und Kirschholz.

La construction de cet appartement a été pensée pour mêler le projet et la ville. Elle avait aussi pour but de gagner sur les quatre façades et le toit, et de créer un décor approprié pour un mobilier et une collection d'architectes et d'artistes XXe. Le niveau inférieur sépare les espaces privés et communs au moyen de sièges et sofas. L'un de ceux-ci est matérialisé par un cercle au sein d'une cage de verre, un double escalier d'acier en colimaçon menant au toit. Le niveau supérieur accueille un séjour intime et un lieu d'exposition. Le projet propose une distribution de l'espace intéressante, recourant à des matériaux tels l'aluminium, le verre trempé blanc et le cerisier.

5th Avenue Duplex
Shelton, Mindel & Associates

Photos: © Michael Moran
Completion date: 2001

The aim of redesigning this dark and horizontally organized pre-war duplex was to make use of its potential vertical space by way of a modernist two-story limestone clad service bar that runs along the length of the duplex. Containing two entries, a stairway, storage space, bathrooms, and a passage, it begins in the living room where the floor slab was eliminated to create a vertical salon with a new double-height window facing the park. Visible from the second story, the bar culminates in the kitchen. A two-story limestone facade in the living room reveals a sweeping staircase, overlooked by the master study above. The steel staircase in the kitchen stands freely against the two-story stone elevation.

Ziel der Neugestaltung dieser dunklen und horizontal ausgerichteten Vorkriegswohnung über zwei Etagen war es, das vertikale Potenzial des Raumes durch ein über zwei Geschosse reichendes, mit Kalkstein verkleidetes Serviceelement zu nutzen, das sich über die Länge des Apartments erstreckt. Es beinhaltet zwei Eingangsöffnungen, eine Treppe, Stauraum, Bäder und einen Korridor, der im Wohnzimmer beginnt. Ein Teil der Deckenplatte wurde entfernt, um einen Salon mit einem über zwei Geschosse reichenden Fenster zum Park zu schaffen. Eine hohe Kalksteinwand im Wohnraum enthüllt eine in weitem Bogen geführte Treppe, die vom Arbeitszimmer überblickt wird. Die Stahltreppe in der Küche durchquert frei den Raum.

Le remodelage de ce duplex avant guerre, sombre et distribué à l'horizontale, devait révéler son potentiel vertical, en s'appuyant sur un comptoir de bar moderniste à deux niveaux, revêtu de combe, et parcourant l'appartement dans sa longueur. Doté de deux entrées, d'un escalier, de rangements, de salles de bain et d'un corridor, il commence dans le séjour où le dallage a été éliminé pour créer un salon ver-tical. Une nouvelle fenêtre à double hauteur fait face au parc. Une façade en combe de deux étages dans le séjour révèle un large escalier, surplombé par le bureau principal. L'escalier d'acier dans la cuisine s'appuie librement sur l'élévation en pierre à deux étages.

Hudson Loft

Moneo Brock

Photos: © Jordi Miralles
Completion date: 2000

A raw warehouse space with nothing but bare walls, massive concrete mushroom columns and huge east-facing windows was transformed into a contemporary home. Made entirely out of concrete, architects experimented with materials that arouse the senses, colors that conserve the clean uncluttered atmosphere, and layers of transparency to ensure the continuous flow of light and space. This is evident in the bathrooms, where beautiful shower structures along with unique lamps give a very specific feeling to the room. At the entrance, an installation of paper-art by Amanda Guest produces a diaphanous translucent skin. Decorative objects like these and warm colors offset the linear qualities of the space.

Für dieses Projekt wurde ein rohes Lagerhaus mit nichts als kahlen Mauern, massiven Betonpfeilern und einem enormen Ostfenster in ein zeitgenössisches Wohnhaus umgestaltet. Der Loft be-steht vollständig aus Beton. Die Architekten experimentierten mit Materialien, welche die Sinne stimulieren, Farben, die das reine, geordnete Ambiente bewahren und transparenten Flächen, die ein kontinuierliches Fließen von Licht und Raum ermöglichen. Das Ergebnis wird besonders deutlich in den Bädern, wo wunderschöne Armaturen und auffällige Lampen dem Raum eine besondere Stimmung verleihen. Weitere Dekorationsobjekte und warme Farben streichen die klaren Umrisse des Raumes heraus.

Ce projet a requis la transformation d'un espace d'entrepôt brut doté de murs nus, de colonnes de béton massif à chapiteau et de larges fenêtres orientées est, en un foyer mo-derne. Le loft a entièrement été réalisé en béton. Les architectes ont expérimenté à l'aide de matériaux stimulant les sens, de couleurs préservant l'atmosphère pure et aérée, et de nappes de transparence assurant la fluidité de la lumière et de l'espace. Avec pour résultat symbolique les salles de bains, où de superbes structures de douche et des lampes exceptionnelles dotent la pièce d'une ambiance spéciale. Dans l'entrée, une installation de paper-art par Amanda Guest produit une membrane translucide et diaphane. D'au-tres objets décoratifs et des couleurs chaudes compensent la nature linéaire de l'espace.

Decorative elements are kept to a minimum. A bold print rug, an elegantly arched lamp, and series of vases are just enough to adorn the living area.

Dekorative Elemente wurden auf ein Minimum beschränkt. Ein kecker bedruckter Teppich, eine elegante gebogene Lampe und mehrere Vasen reichen aus, um den Wohnraum zu schmücken.

Les éléments décoratifs ont été réduits au minimum. Un tapis imprimé en relief, une élégante lampe en cloche, et une série de vases suffisent à embellir le séjour.

Moneo Loft

Moneo Brock

Photos: © Jordi Miralles
Completion date: 1997

The architect´s studio and home lies on the tenth and top floor of an 1898 warehouse building in Tribeca. Its low ceilings, triangular plan, tight column grid, and low hanging pipes presented the main difficulties. The solution was to open the roof in strategic locations, and to use the columns as orientative elements that divide the space into working and living areas. The studio skylight and glass wall permit views of the building´s rooftop water tanks while emphasizing the loft´s vertical dimensions. Transparency, color, and storage space are key elements within the design. The bedroom is also skylit and the bathrooms are finished in unglazed ceramic tiles in blocks of four different colors.

Atelier und Heim des Architekten liegen in Tribeca im zehnten und obersten Stock eines Lagerhauses von 1898. Seine niedrigen Decken, der dreieckige Grundriss, das enge Säulennetz sowie tief hängende Rohre stellten große Herausforderungen dar. Die Lösung besteht darin, das Dach an strategischen Punkten zu öffnen und die Säulen als Orientierungspunkte zu nutzen, die den Raum in Wohn- und Arbeitsbereiche aufteilen. Das Oberlicht und die Glasfassade des Arbeitszimmers bieten Ausblicke auf die Wassertanks auf dem Dach des Gebäudes. Das Schlafzimmer erhält ebenfalls Tageslicht von oben, und die Badezimmer sind mit unglasierten Keramikfliesen in unterschiedlichen Farben ausgelegt.

Le studio/foyer de l'architecte est situé au dixième et dernier étage d'un entrepôt de Tribeca, de 1898. Plafonds bas, plan triangulaire, quadrillage étroit de colonnes et tuyauterie apparente constituaient les principaux défis. La réponse: ouvrir le toit en des endroits stratégiques, et utiliser les colonnes comme éléments d'orientation divisant l'espace en aires de travail et de séjour. La lucarne et le mur vitré de l'étude offrent des vues sur la citerne située sur le toit, et accentuent les dimensions verticales du loft. La chambre dispose aussi d'une lucarne, les salles de bains s'ornant de carreaux céramiques mats de quatre couleurs.

INTERIOR DESIGN

ROBERT MORRIS
JOSEF FRANK
UTAMARO
OTEIZA

The rooms display an unrestricted mix of patterns and colors. The child´s room breathes a carefree spirit that reverberates throughout the entire household.

Die Räume stellen einen unbegrenzten Muster- und Farbenmix zur Schau. Das Kinderzimmer atmet einen sorglosen Geist, der im ganzen Haushalt zu spüren ist.

Les pièces affichent un mélange illimité de motifs et de couleurs. La chambre d'enfant insuffle un esprit d'insouciance qui s'étend dans toute la maison.

Dr. Heong Residence

Kar-Hwa Ho

Photos: © Björg
Completion date: 1999
kho@kbf.com

The objectives for remodeling this space were to upgrade the quality of its interior, to give the space a greater and more cohesive structure, and to create a sense of calm and repose. The windows along the north bank are sheathed in sunshades that thread the rooms together. Wooden wall panels create full height storage doors with an integrated picture rail. Planar qualities are emphasized by base and ceiling reveals and recessed switch plates and outlets. The dark wood floors contrast with the lightness of the walls and the discreet touches of bold color. The upholstery offers a variety of tactile sensations, a feature that stands out among the subdued restraint of the architectural palette.

Ziel der Renovierung war es, die Qualität des Innenraums zu steigern, dem Raum eine größere und geschlossenere Struktur zu geben und den Eindruck von Ruhe und Erholung zu vermitteln. Die Fenster entlang der Nordflanke sind mit Sonnenblenden verhüllt. Türen aus Holzpaneelen verbergen raumhohen Stauraum und haben integrierte Bilderschienen. Ebene Flächen werden durch Schattenkanten an Böden und Decken, vertiefte Schalternischen und Abzüge hervorgehoben. Die dunklen Holzböden kontrastieren mit der Helligkeit der Wände und Markisen sowie mit den diskreten Farbtupfern. Die Polstermöbel bieten verschiedenste Sinneseindrücke, ein Merkmal, das aus der zurückhaltenden Palette der Architektur heraussticht.

La réorganisation de cet espace avait pour but d'enrichir la nature de son intérieur, de lui fournir une structure plus puissante et cohérente, et de créer une sensation de calme et de détente. Les fenêtres du côté nord sont gainées de pare-soleil qui relient les pièces entre-elles. Des panneaux de bois créent des portes de placard pleine hauteur, avec une cimaise intégrée. La planéité est rehaussée par les reliefs du sol et du plafond, et par les interrupteurs et prises de courants encastrés. Les parquets sombres contrastent avec la clarté des murs et des stores, et une discrète touche de couleur plus audacieuse. La tapisserie offre une variété de sensations tactiles, élément de différenciation dans une palette architectural plus retenue.

Custom furnishings were selected for its clean lines and simple forms. Most light is indirect and decoration is subtle.

Die nach Wunsch des Kunden gefertigten Möbel wurden wegen ihrer reinen Linien und schlichten Form gewählt. Die Beleuchtung ist hauptsächlich indirekt, die Dekoration subtil.

L'ameublement sur mesure a été choisi pour ses lignes pures et ses formes simples. La lumière est essentiellement indirecte, et la décoration subtile.

Flatiron Loft

Kar-Hwa Ho

Photos: © Björg
Completion date: 1998
kho@kbf.com

Inside an old warehouse next to the Empire State Building, this loft was designed to maintain its diaphanous quality. The original distribution was preserved, and features were introduced to promote serenity and comfort. Light panels line the walls, and most of the interior, including the doors, is a luminous creme. The glass bar is an original and colorful element that visually joins the kitchen and the dining area. There is abundant storage space and air conditioning was installed discreetly so as to harmonize with the existing design. Doorknobs are incorporated into the walls, and the charm of this spacious and flexible home comes from such clever details.

In einem alten Lagerhaus nahe dem Empire State Building wurde dieser Loft so gestaltet, dass er seinen offenen Charakter bewahren konnte. Die ursprüngliche Raumanordnung wurde beibehalten und neue Elemente fördern die Behaglichkeit. Lichtschienen verlaufen parallel zu den Wänden und die Einrichtung, einschließlich der Türen, ist hell cremefarben. Die gläserne Bar ist ein farbenfrohes Element, das Küche und Essbereich optisch verbindet. Es gibt viel Stauraum, und die Klimaanlage ist diskret, so dass sie das Design nicht stört. Die Türöffner befinden sich in der Wand – derartig clevere Details machen den Charme dieser geräumigen, wandelbaren Wohnung aus.

Dans un vieil entrepôt proche de l'Empire State Building, ce loft a été conçu pour conserver sa nature diaphane. L'organisation originelle a été préservée et des caractéristiques nouvelles introduites pour instaurer sérénité et confort. Des panneaux de lumière sillonnent les murs, la majeure partie de l'intérieur, portes inclues, étant d'un crème lumineux. Élément original et pittoresque, le bar en verre associe visuellement la cuisine et l'aire de repas. L'espace de rangement est généreux et l'installation d'air conditionné discrète pour s'accorder avec le design existant. Les poignées de portes s'encastrent dans les murs, le charme de ce foyer spacieux et souple naissant de ces détails astucieux.

Loft

Kar-Hwa Ho

Photos: © Björg
Completion date: 1996
kho@kbf.com

This loft offers a flexible layout of space enhanced by materials and objects that create luminosity and a feeling of repose. Although areas like the master bedroom and bathroom are visually isolated from the living room, office, kitchen, and dining area, there is no partition that rigidly defines the borders between them. Divisions are established through transparency based on layers of translucent materials, sandblasted matte glass, and indirect lighting. In the bathroom, the lack of windows led to the introduction of mirrors, treated glass, and limestone, rendering an elegant and intimate feel. Piles of books on shelves, curious objects, warm colors, and curvy furniture contribute to a homely and unrestrained atmosphere.

Dieser Loft präsentiert ein flexibles Raumdesign, das durch Materialien und Objekte, die für Helligkeit und Entspanntheit sorgen, aufgewertet wurde. Obwohl Schlafzimmer und Bad optisch von Wohnzimmer, Arbeitsraum, Küche und Essplatz isoliert sind, gibt es doch keine Trennwände, die die Grenzen festsetzen würden. Stattdessen besteht eine transparente Unterteilung durch Scheiben aus durchscheinendem, sandgestrahlten Glas und indirekter Beleuchtung. Da das Bad keine Fenster hat, wurden Spiegel, speziell behandeltes Glas und Kalkstein eingesetzt, die eine elegante und private Stimmung auslösen. Bücherstapel auf den Regalen, Kuriosa, warme Farben und runde Möbel tragen zur heimeligen und offenen Atmosphäre bei.

Ce loft offre une disposition souple de l'espace, rehaussée par des matériaux et des objets apportant luminosité et sensation de détente. Bien que la chambre principale et la salle de bain soient visuellement isolées du séjour, du bureau, de la cuisine et de la salle à manger, aucune cloison ne fixe strictement les limites entre ces zones. La séparation s'établit plutôt par transparence, reposant sur des strates de matériaux translucides, de verre mat sablé et sur l'éclairage indirect. Dans la salle de bain, l'absence de fenêtres a requis l'introduction de miroirs, de verre traité et de combe créant une sensation de raffinement et d'intimité. Livres empilés sur des étagères, objets rares, couleurs chaudes et mobilier curviligne engendrent une atmosphère libre et familiale.

GIO PONTI

Two pillars define the living/dining/kitchen area.
The bedroom/office is open plan, parted from the main area
and forms a space of its own.

Zwei Pfeiler umreißen die Wohn-/Ess-/Kochzone.
Das kombinierte offene Schlaf-/Arbeitszimmer ist vom Hauptteil
der Wohnung abgeteilt und bildet einen eigenen Bereich.

Deux piliers délimitent l'aire séjour/repas/cuisine.
Le bureau/chambre est un plan ouvert, séparé de l'aire principale,
et forme un espace à part.

Chelsea Loft

Kar-Hwa Ho

Photos: © Björg
Completion date: 1996
kho@kbf.com

The primary goal of architect Kar-Hwa Ho and designer Susanna Sirefman in creating this project was to take full advantage of as much exterior light as possible and to develop a fluid space that would define and separate the public and private zones. To achieve this end, translucent glass and an efficient system of artificial lighting were used to endow the space with homogenous illumination and depth. The selected furniture defines the borders between different areas, as do mobile structures. A neutral palette and dark floors unify all the elements. The spaces remain visually linked but are perceptually individual. Design details distinguish the various zones and create a relaxed and traquil atmosphere.

Das Hauptziel des Architekten Kar-Hwa Ho und der Designerin Susanna Sirefman war es, das Tageslicht maximal auszunutzen; gleichzeitig wollten sie einen fließenden Raum entwickeln, der öffentliche und private Bereiche definiert und voneinander abtrennt. Aus diesem Grund wurde der Raum mit durchscheinendem Glas und einer effizienten Beleuchtung gleichmäßig erhellt. Die ausgewählte Möblierung sowie bewegliche Elemente ziehen Grenzen zwischen den verschiedenen Bereichen. Neutrale Farben und dunkle Böden vereinen alle Elemente: Die Räume bleiben optisch verknüpft, werden jedoch für sich wahrgenommen. Design-Details markieren einzelne Bereiche und schaffen eine ruhige, entspannte Atmosphäre.

En créant ce projet, l'architecte Kar-Hwa Ho et la designer Susanna Sirefman avaient pour but principal de profiter pleinement de la lumière extérieure, et de développer un espace fluide définissant et séparant les aires privées et communes. À cet effet, ils ont eu recours au verre translucide et à un système efficace de lumière artificielle pour doter l'espace d'une illumination et d'une profondeur homogènes. Le mobilier, choisi, et les structures mobiles signifient les limites entre les différents espaces. Une palette neutre et des sols sombres unifient tous les éléments. Les espaces sont visuellement liés mais perceptiblement individualisés. Des détails de design permettent de distinguer diverses aires, créant une atmosphère détendue et tranquille.

At the entrance, a false ceiling lit from above spreads indirect light. Boundaries between areas are delineated by furniture.

Im Eingangsbereich streut die von oben beleuchtete eingezogene Decke indirektes Licht. Möbelstücke ziehen die Grenzen zwischen einzelnen Bereichen.

Dans l'entrée, un faux plafond illuminé par le haut dispense une lumière indirecte. Le mobilier dessine les limites entre les espaces.

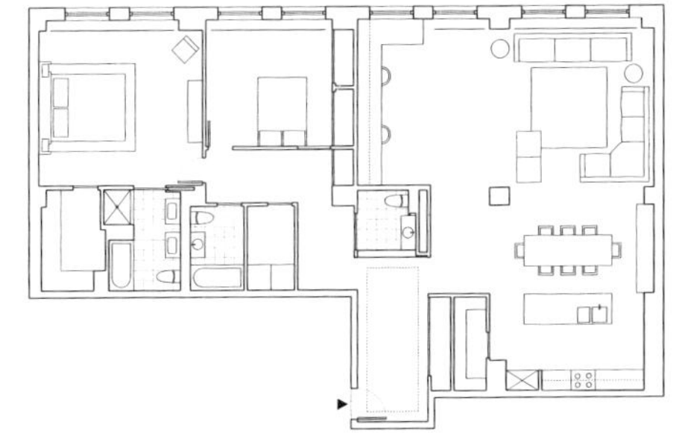

Abell Residence

1100 Architect

Photos: © Michael Moran
Completion date: 1998
contact@1100architect.com
www.1100architect.com

The primary objective in the design of this downtown Manhattan residence was the integration of two separate and distinct floors to form one coherent space. The spiral staircase and lightwell unify the apartment in a continuous flowing gesture, while also suggesting a space sculpted by water. The apartment reflects the design philosophy of both the client and the architect. The client, an avid outdoorsman, sought to bring the complexity and serenity experienced in nature into his home. Dark wood, blue floors and crisp white walls predominate. The minimalist master bedroom suite interprets and redefines his previous home in Asia, with its floor-level bed, series of floor mats, and sliding translucent panels.

Das vorherrschende Element ist die Wendeltreppe mit ihrem Licht/Luftraum, der die beiden Etagen in einer durchgehenden, fließenden Bewegung verbindet. Sie ist ein optisches Highlight, das die Grenzen zwischen Gesellschafts- und privaten Bereichen zieht. Die Kurvenform vermittelt den Eindruck eines von Wasser geformten Raumes. Als Naturliebhaber strebte der Kunde danach, die in der Natur vorkommende Schlichtheit nachzubilden. Dunkle Holzböden und solide Holzmöbel harmonieren mit ozeanblauen Fußböden und blendend weißen Wänden. Das Schlafzimmer bietet einen Hauch von asiatischem Minimalismus mit einem Bett zu ebener Erde, mehreren Bodenmatten und beweglichen lichtdurchlässigen Paneelen.

La caractéristique prédominante de ce lieu aéré est l'escalier en colimaçon/puits de lumière, reliant les deux niveaux d'un seul mouvement fluide. L'escalier est un élément visuel fort, qui délimite aussi les domaines des espaces publics et privés. Il reflète la philosophie conceptuelle de l'architecte, sa forme courbée suggérant un espace sculpté par l'eau. Passionné d'environnement, le client a cherché à recréer dans sa maison la serénité rencontrée dans la nature. Parquets sombres et mobilier de bois massif s'harmonisent avec des sols bleu océan et des murs blanc vif. La chambre principale offre une touche asiatique minimaliste: lit à même le sol, ensemble de nattes, et panneaux coulissants translucides.

Rifkin Loft

1100 Architect

Photos: © Michael Moran
Completion date: 1997
contact@1100architect.com
www.1100architect.com

This downtown loft was designed to emphasize the unobstructed views of lower Manhattan, making the cityscape an integral part of the home. A clean and simple space serves as the backdrop for the client´s artwork and their eclectic collection of antique European and modern American furniture. A multitude of unique and peculiar decorative objects adorn the household, adding color and personal style. The U-shaped floor plan allows rooms to flow into one another and provides the option of closing off a room or leaving it open for a larger sense of space. A continuous concrete ledge along the walls serves as a windowsill and as a visual connection between the windows and walls.

Die Exzentrik der Stadt reflektierend, ist dieses Wohnhaus eine kostbare Mischung aus antikem europäischen sowie modernem amerikanischen Mobiliar, eigentümlichen Schmuckstücken und bunten Kunstwerken. Weit entfernt vom Minimalismus, ist die Wohnung mit einer Viel-zahl wie zufällig arrangierter Objekte angefüllt. Grün- und Orangetöne dominieren ge-genüber weißen Wänden und Holzböden. Der Grund-riss in Form eines U lässt die Räume ineinander fließen und lässt die Wahl, einen bestimmten Bereich zu öffnen oder zu verschließen. Ei-ne durchgehende Fensterbank aus Beton wurde entlang der Wände angebracht, um eine horizontale Linie zu ziehen, die mit den soliden vertikalen Flächen zusammenspielt.

Reflétant la complexité et l'excentricité de sa ville, cette résidence est un mélange luxueux de mobiliers européens anciens et américains modernes, de bibelots bizarres et d'œuvres d'art pittoresques. Loin du minimalisme, le lieu héberge une multitude d'objets soigneusement placés au hasard. Verts et orange prédominent contre des murs blancs et des parquets de bois. L'espace en forme de U permet aux chambres de toutes s'imbriquer, et offre l'option d'ouvrir ou fermer une zone spécifique. Un rebord continu en béton a été placé le long des murs, sous les fenêtres, pour créer une ligne horizontale interagissant avec les plans verticaux dominants. Cette demeure et sa collection de pièces uniques et originales offrent une stimulation visuelle sans fin.

Upper East Side Apartment

1100 Architect

Photos: © Michael Moran
Completion date: 1997
contact@1100architect.com
www.1100architect.com

This apartment was transformed into a modern residence that reflects the owner's lifestyle and showcases their extensive contempo-rary art collection. The vestibule was removed and combined with the hall and foyer to form an informal art gallery. The living and dining room were combined into one space and connected to the gallery with two large steel and frosted glass sliding doors. The kitchen, maid´s room and bath were joined with the kitchen/living area. The new layout provides multi-prupose social spaces with sliding doors that offer privacy when closed. All that remains from the original space is the herringbone patterned wood flooring—in its place is a contemporary residence with a downtown atmosphere.

Die Umstrukturierung dieser Vorkriegswohnung führte zu ihrer Verwandlung in ein zeitgenössisches Innenstadt-Apartment. Der Architekt öffnete einzelne Bereiche, um verschiedene Ambiente zu kombinieren und eine beeindruckende Sammlung zeitgenössischer Kunst auszustellen. Das Foyer wurde entfernt und mit der Vorhalle zu einem Ausstellungsraum verschmolzen. Zwei große Schiebetüren aus Stahl und Milchglas verbinden den Wohn- und Essraum, und eine neue erweiterte Küche ist Teil des Aufenthaltsraumes. Schiebetüren und multifunktionelle Räume lassen die Wahl zwischen Gesellschafts- und privaten Umgebungen. Einzig die Holzböden mit Fischgratmuster blieben vom ursprünglichen Raum erhalten.

La reconfiguration de cet appartement d'avant guerre a abouti à sa transformation en une résidence moderne du centre ville. L'architecte a ouvert certaines zones pour unir les atmosphères, et présenter une collection d'art moderne spectaculaire. Le vestibule a disparu, se fondant avec le hall et la réception pour servir de galerie. Deux grandes portes coulissantes en acier et verre dépoli réunissent séjour et salle à manger, la nouvelle cuisine agrandie s'incorporant au salon. Portes à glissière et espaces multifonctions offrent un choix entre les environnements public et privé, un nuancier de couleurs gaies donnant vie à ce projet. Le seul élément originel finalement conservé est le parquet en chevrons.

Midtown Penthouse

Gates Merkulova Architects

Photos: © Gates Merkulova Architects
Completion date: 2000
paul@gmarch.com
www.gmarch.com

This penthouse loft is wrapped by windows on all four sides affording close-up views of such midtown landmarks as the Empire State Building. Designed for an accomplished amateur musician who wanted a space where he could play for himself and his guests, this previously compartmentalized space was recon-figured to emit a sense of light and ex-panse. Mobile planes made of translucent laminated glass and high-gloss aircraft paint screen off the broad living area from the kitchen and storage areas, while the bedrooms are kept private thanks to a long hallway. White maple floors, ebonized ceiling-height room doors, and raw steel structural supports enhance the abstract complexion of this modern space.

Fenster nach allen Seiten bieten in diesem Penthouse-Loft Ausblick auf die nah gelegenen Wahrzeichen wie Empire State und New York Life Building. Für einen Musiker, der Platz brauchte, um für sich und seine Gäste spielen zu können, wurde der ehemals dunkle und zersplitterte Raum umstrukturiert, um den Eindruck von Licht und Weite zu vermitteln. Bewegliche Wandschirme aus durchscheinendem Schichtglas und extrem glänzender Flugzeugfarbe schirmen den offenen Wohnraum von der Küche und den Stauräumen ab. Die Schlafzimmer sind dank eines langen Flures dem Privatleben vorbehalten. Weiße Ahornholzböden, raumhohe schwarze Türen und rohe Stahlträger verstärken den abstrakten Anstrich dieses modernen Raums.

Ce loft en penthouse est revêtu de fenêtres sur ses quatre côtés, offrant des plans rapprochés sur des éléments du centre-ville aussi éminents que l'Empire State Building et le New York Life Building. Conçu pour un musicien amateur émérite, souhaitant un espace pour partager sa musique, ce lieu jadis sombre et compartimenté a été redistribué pour susciter une sensation de lu-mière et de volume. Des plans mobiles en verre feuilleté translucide et de nombreux écrans au brillant éclatant, ouvrent l'aire de séjour sur les coins cuisine et rangement. La tranquillité des chambres est préservée grâce à un long couloir. Parquets en érable blanc, portes noir ébène à hauteur de plafond et supports structurels en acier brut rehaussent la nature abstraite de cet espace moderne.

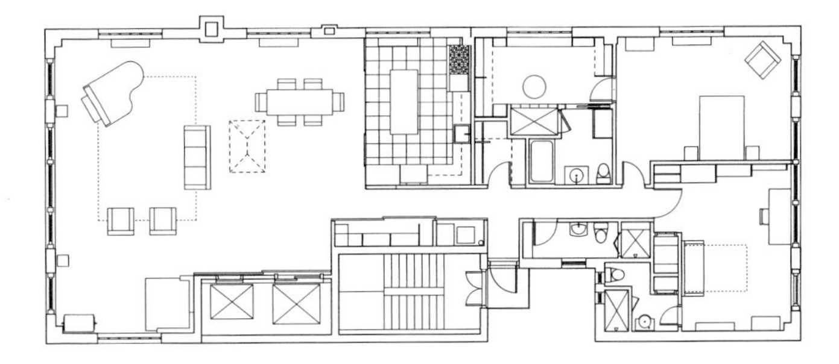

Weil Townhouse

Gates Merkulova Architects

Photos: © J.B. Grant
Completion date: 1999
paul@gmarch.com
www.gmarch.com

This 18th century townhouse was in such a state of disrepair that a complete reconstruction was imperative. A new structure was inserted into the three masonry walls and the street facade was restored to its historic character. The main entrance became an unexpectedly modern surface of taught aluminum and glass skin. Uncommon to most New York houses, the main entrance to the townhouse is found at the rear, where a private courtyard is enclosed by vine-covered walls. Each floor was treated as a loft to optimize space and flexibility using translucent materials and sliding partitions. A spiral staircase surrounded by the owner's artwork leads up to the roof terrace and private garden.

Das Haus aus dem 18. Jahrhundert musste komplett überholt werden. In die alten Mauern wurde eine neue Struktur eingebaut, während die Fassade zur Straße restauriert wurde, um den historischen Charakter zu bewahren. Als Kontrast dazu wurde der Haupteingang mit einer unerwartet modernen Oberfläche aus gespanntem Aluminium und Glas gestaltet. Er befindet sich im Gegensatz zu den meisten New Yorker Häusern hinter dem Haus, wo sich ein privater Garten, eingeschlossen von mit Wein überrankten Mauern, anschließt. Da das Haus klein ist, wurde jede Etage wie ein Loft gestaltet, um Raum und Flexibilität durch transparente Materialien und bewegliche Raumteiler zu optimieren. Eine Wendeltreppe führt auf die begrünte Dachterrasse.

L'état de délabrement de cet hôtel particulier XVIIIe a imposé une refonte complète. Une nouvelle charpente a été insérée dans les trois murs porteurs, et la façade restaurée à l'original. En contrepoint, l'entrée principale est devenue contre toute attente une surface moderne d'aluminium et de verre. Contrairement à la plupart des foyers new-yorkais, l'entrée se trouve à l'arrière, dans une cour privée entourée de murs couverts de vignes. La maison étant petite, chaque niveau est traité comme un loft, pour optimiser l'espace et la modularité, avec des matériaux translucides et des cloisons coulissantes. Un escalier en colimaçon encadré d'œuvres d'art du propriétaire - de grandes diapositives dans des panneaux de verre - mène à la terrasse sur le toit et au jardin.

The staircase is flanked by large transparencies inserted between glass panels that feature the owner´s beautiful images of magnified leaves. The front door looks out on the private courtyard rather than a busy street.

Die Treppe wird von großen Folien zwischen Glasscheiben eingerahmt; es sind wunderbare Bilder des Eigentümers von vergrößerten Blättern. Die Eingangstür blickt auf den privaten Hof und nicht wie sonst häufig auf eine belebte Straße.

L'escalier est encadré de grandes diapositives, proposant les magnifiques images de feuilles agrandies du propiétaire, insérées dans des panneaux de verre. La porte principale donne sur la cour privée, plutôt que sur une rue animée.

WEST ELEVATION

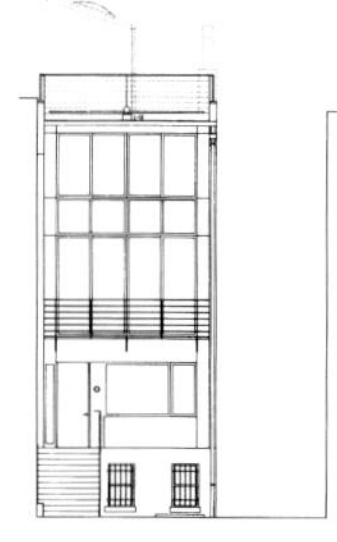

EAST ELEVATION

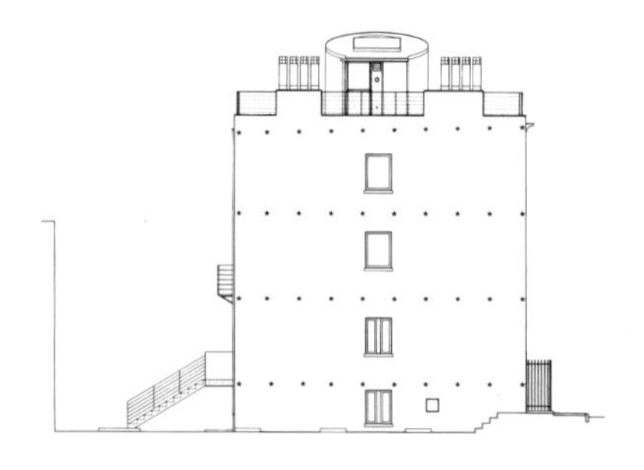

NORTH ELEVATION

Levine Loft

Gates Merkulova Architects

Photos: © Gates Merkulova Architects
Completion date: 1998
paul@gmarch.com
www.gmarch.com

The design goal of this SoHo loft was to create an easy, flexible space for a bachelor who is both an accomplished cook and an avid collector of Japanese furniture. The ceilings are tall, and large windows cover two sides of the apartment. The open living area communicates with the kitchen, which features laminated translucent glass, sandblasted stainless steel, and cast resin laboratory counters whose refined finish softens their industrial hardness. The sleeping area can be either screened off or linked to the main space by way of oversized sliding partitions. The study also doubles as a guestroom. The modern installations offer an attractive contrast to the owner's beautiful rugs and Oriental furnishings.

Dieser SoHo-Loft sollte ein leichter, anpassungsfähger Raum für einen Junggesellen sein, der sowohl vielseitiger Koch als auch passionierter Sammler japanischer Möbel ist. Die Decken sind hoch und breite Fenster öffnen zwei Seiten des Apartments. Offener Wohnraum und Küche sind eins; die Küche ist mit durchscheinendem mehrschichtigen Glas, sandgestrahltem Edelstahl und einer aus Harz gegossenen Theke, deren raffiniertes Finish den industriellen Look ausgleicht, ausgestattet. Der Schlafbereich kann mittels Schiebeflächen verborgen oder mit dem Hauptraum verbunden und das Büro in ein Gästezimmer verwandelt werden. Die modernen Installationen stellen ein attraktives Gegengewicht zu den Teppichen und orientalischen Möbeln dar.

La conception de ce loft de Soho avait pour but de créer un espace commode et flexible pour un célibataire, cuisinier consommé et collectionneur de mobilier japonais. Les plafonds sont hauts, et de grandes fenêtres couvrent deux côtés de l'appartement. L'aire des séjour, ouverte, communique avec la cuisine, proposant verre feuilleté translucide, acier dépoli et comptoirs en résine, dont la finition raffinée adoucit la sévérité industrielle. L'aire de repos peut être soit cachée, soit reliée à l'espace principal par des cloisons coulissantes surdimensionnées. L'étude sert aussi de chambre d'hôte. Les équipements modernes offrent un contraste séduisant aux splendides tapis et accessoires orientaux du propriétaire.

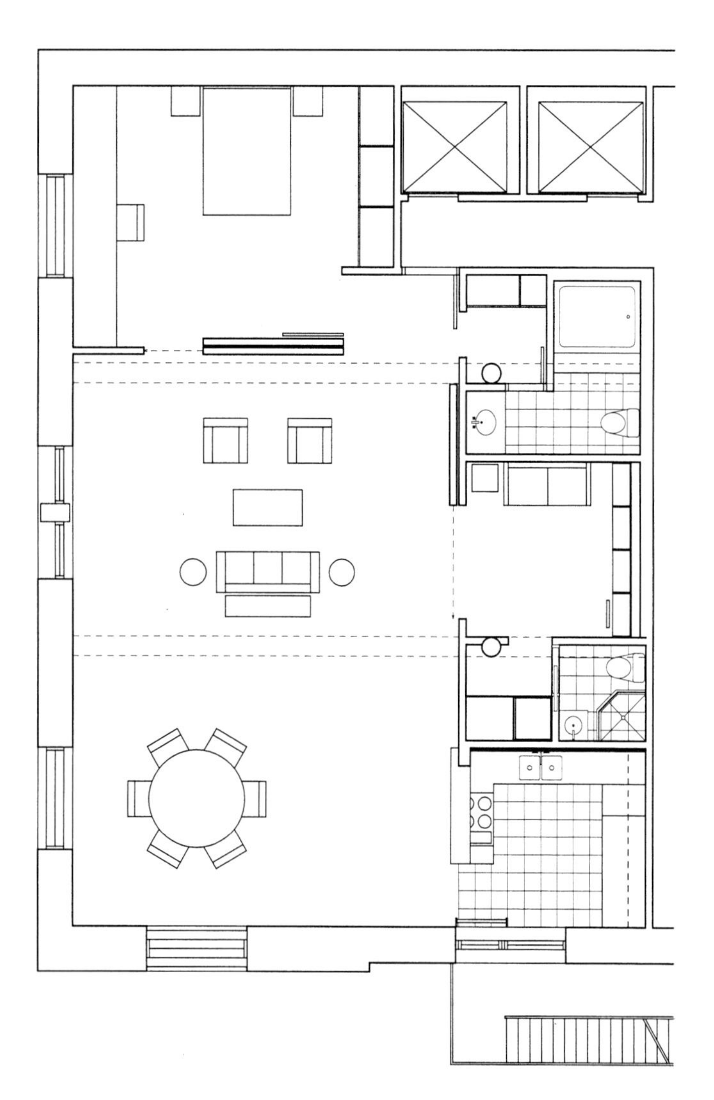

Davol loft

Moneo Brock

Photos: © Michael Moran
Completion date: 1999
www.hhpa.com

Designed for a pair of professional musicians, this empty rectangular space was partitioned into two bedrooms with attached bathrooms, a kitchen, a small storage room, and a flexible work area for each. The di-viders, made of a new material called Panelite, were a critical element in the overall feel of the space. Panelite´s translucent and light sensitive nature casts different colors at different times of the day. The dividers are independent from the ceiling and their mobility allows for diverse spatial relationships and the redistribution of space. The key to this irides-cent metropolitan palace was the architect´s imagination and the clients´willingness to risk the use of low budget and experimental materials.

Dieser Loft wurde für ein Musikerpaar gestaltet. Der leere rechteckige Raum wurde in zwei Schlafzimmer mit angeschlossenen Bädern, eine Küche, einen kleinen Abstellraum und einen flexiblen Arbeitsbereich für jeden der Bewohner gegliedert. Die Raumteiler, aus einem neuen Material namens Panelite, sind eines der wesentlichsten Elemente der Raumatmosphäre. Es ist durchscheinend und nimmt im Verlauf der Tageszeiten unterschiedliche Färbungen an. Die Raumteiler sind nicht fixiert, ihre Beweglichkeit ermöglicht neue Einteilungen des Lofts. Der Schlüssel zu diesem schillernden Palast lag in der Vorstellungskraft des Architekten und der Risikobereitschaft des Kunden kostengünstige und experimentelle Materialien einzusetzen.

Ce loft fut conçu pour un couple de musiciens professionnels. L'espace rectangulaire vide a été divisé en deux chambres avec salles de bain attenantes, une cuisine, une petite pièce de rangement et une aire de travail flexible pour chacun des occupants. Les séparations, d'un nouveau matériau appelé Panelite, ont été un élément essentiel dans l'appréhension globale de l'espace. La nature translucide et photosensible du Panelite projette des couleurs différentes selon le moment de la journée. Les cloisons sont indépendantes du plafond et leur mobilité permet diverses relations spatiales et une redistribution de l'espace. Éléments clés de ce palaismulticolore, l'imagination de l'architecte et la volonté du client d'utiliser des matériaux bon marché et expérimentaux.

Architect´s Residence

Hardy Holzman Pfeiffer Associates

Photos: © Hardy Holzman Pfeiffer Associates
Completion date: 1998
www.hhpa.com

This 12th floor apartment is surrounded by some of the city's most renowned architecture by architects like Burnham, Corbett, and Hardenberg. During the renovation, the dilapidated state of the beams and ceilings was conserved to display the installations of the original freight elevator. The skylight was replaced with new translucent glass true to the period of the building's construction, and the pavement was polished and tinted a dark red. Fine undulated panels of fiberglass acquire a transparency and shine thanks to the interior fluorescent lighting. Paintings, rugs, furniture, and other objects of contrasting styles and different periods enhance this eclectic and stimulating residence.

Dieses Appartment im 12. Stock liegt im historischen Kern New Yorks und ist von einigen der bekanntesten Bauwerke von Architekten wie Burnham, Corbett und Hardenberg umgeben. Bei der Renovierung wurde der baufällige Zustand der Träger und Decken konserviert, um die Installationen des alten Lastenaufzugs offen zu legen. Ein Oberlicht wurde entsprechend der ursprünglichen Konstruktionsweise neu verglast, der Boden poliert und dunkelrot gefärbt. Zart gewellte Glasfaserpaneele werden transparent und leuchten dank der installierten Neonröhren. Bilder, Teppiche, Möbel und andere Objekte verschiedenster Stilrichtungen und Epochen geben der exzentrischen und anregenden Behausung den letzten Schliff.

Cet appartement, situé au 12e au centre du New York historique, est entouré des œuvres d'architectes tel Burnham, Corbett et Hardenberg, parmi les plus renommées de la ville. Au cours de la rénovation, l'état délabré des piliers et plafonds a été préservé pour exposer les installations du monte-charge originel. La lucarne a été remplacée par un verre translucide respectant le style de l'époque de construction, et le carrelage poli et teinté de rouge foncé. Des panneaux finement ondulés en fibre de verre deviennent transparents et lumineux grâce un éclairage intérieur fluorescent. Tableaux, tapis, meubles et autres objets de styles contrastés et de périodes diverses rehaussent cette résidence excentrique et stimulante.

DRINK
BLATZ
BEER

Central Park Apartment

Pasanella Klein Stolzman + Berg

Photos: © Paul Warchol
Completion date: 1998
lubatkin@pksb.com

A fully renovated and furnished 950-square foot, one-bedroom apartment with terraces overlooking Central Park, this flat's design is inspired by the client's passion for collecting baseball cards. Using baseball as a metaphor, the architects used materials like canvas, steel, stained wood and leather to visualize the apartment as a stadium and Central Park as the field. The bedroom features canvas-stretched sliding panels laced by thin strips of leather to the stainless steel frames.Oval tabletops take precedence over conventional rectangular surfaces. A display case exhibits an exclusive baseball card collection along shelves illuminated under mini strip lighting.

Das Design dieses komplett renovierten und neumöblierten 88 m^2 Apartments mit einem Schlafzimmer und Terrassen mit Blick auf den Central Park wurde von der Baseballkarten-Sammelleidenschaft des Bauherrn inspiriert. Der Architekt bezog sich auf Baseball als Metapher und verwandte Materialien wie Segeltuch, Stahl, buntes Holz und Leder, um das Apartment als Stadion und Central Park als Spielfeld darzustellen. Im Schlafzimmer gibt es mit Stoff bespannte Wandschirme, die mit Lederbändern in Stahlrahmen geknüpft sind. Der Wohnraum unten öffnet sich über raumbreite Edelstahlstufen auf die Terrasse. In einer Vitrine wird die exklusive Baseballkartensammlung auf mit Strahlern beleuchteten Regalen ausgestellt.

Cet appartement d'une chambre, avec terrasses sur Central Park, a été complètement rénové et meublé en s'inspirant de la passion du client pour la collection de cartes de base-ball. Utilisant la métaphore du base-ball, les architectes ont employé des matériaux tels la toile, l'acier, le bois moiré et le cuir visualisant l'appartement comme un stade, et Central Park comme un terrain. La chambre propose des panneaux coulissants tendus de toile, liés par de fins rubans de cuir au cadre d'acier. L'ovale des tables s'impose aux surfaces rectangulaires plus traditionnelles. Plus bas, le séjour accède à la terrasse par de larges marches en acier. Une vitrine expose une collection de cartes exceptionelle, le long d'étagères illuminées par un petit néon.

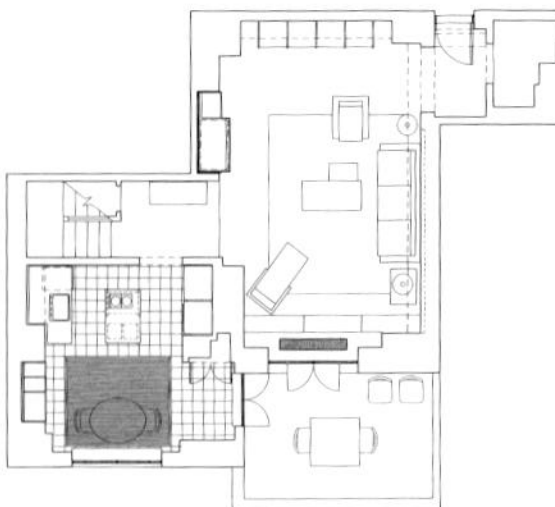

Downtown Loft

Pasanella Klein Stolzman + Berg

Photos: © Paul Warchol
Completion date: 1999
lubatkin@pksb.com

Home to a privileged bachelor, this loft-like space holds a multitude of switches and gadgets that spoil the senses. The space is divided by white-framed translucent glass panels into a separate bedroom, den, and workout/guest room. Wide windows offer views of Madison Square Park's green oval gardens. The interiors are luxurious yet restrained. Some rich teak pieces of furniture are framed in bronze and covered in delicate fabrics. The exclusive bathroom, more like a personal spa resort, is an extravagant play between fiber-optic lights, tinted steam, and jet streams that bubble in unison with the bather's choice of music. And just in case of company, a double-headed over-sized shower for two.

Als Zuhause eines privilegierten Junggesellen hält dieser loftartige Raum eine Vielzahl reizvoller Veränderungsmöglichkeiten und Extras bereit. Der Raum wird durch weißgerahmte semitransparente Glasscheiben in ein Schlafzimmer, Studio und Fitnessraum/Gästezimmer gegliedert. Die Einrichtung ist luxuriös, aber zurückhaltend. Einige kostbare Möbelstücke aus Teak sind in Bronze gerahmt und mit edlen Stoffen bezogen. Das exklusive Badezimmer, fast eher ein privates Freizeitbad, ist ein extravagantes Spiel mit Glasfaserlampen, gefärbtem Dampf und Düsen, die im Takt der Lieblingsmusik des Badenden blubbern. Und für den Fall, dass man nicht alleine ist: eine doppelköpfige Dusche für zwei.

Foyer d'un célibataire fortuné, cet espace/loft abrite une multitude d'interrupteurs et de gadgets, qui stimulent nos sens. Des panneaux de verre translucide encadrés de blanc divisent l'espace en chambre, étude et salle d'exercice/chambre d'hôte. De larges fenêtres offrent des perspectives sur les jardins du parc de Madison Square. Les intérieurs sont d'un luxe tout en retenue. Quelques riches meubles en teck sont ornés de bronze, recouverts de broderie fine. Unique, la salle de bain, plutôt une station thermale personnelle, est un jeu extravagant entre lumières en fibre optique, vapeur colorée et jets d'eau bouillonnants à l'unisson de la musique choisie par le baigneur. Si vous êtes accompagné, la douche a un double pommeau.

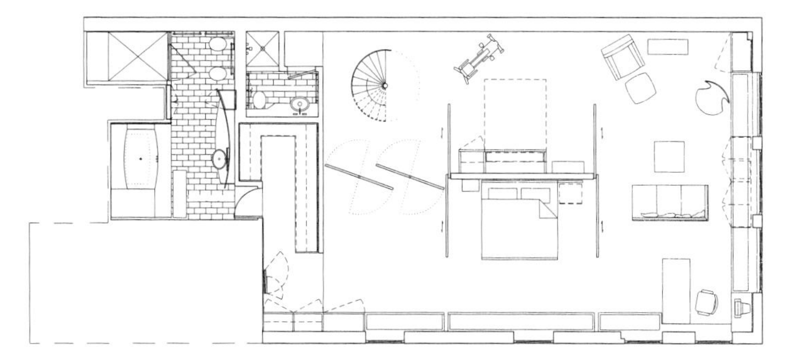

Central Park West Apartment

Pasanella Klein Stolzman + Berg

Photos: © Chuck Choi
Completion date: 1996
lubatkin@pksb.com

This stripped out turn-of-the-century apartment was more disorganized than diaphanous. Architects wanted to bring back the sense of a formal entrance and a logical structure, without returning to the original state. An elliptical foyer was built, and a hallway was reestablished by means of a series of stripped structural columns and a 35-foot long suspended metallic canopy with spotlights illuminating the ceiling and the ebony-stained wood floors. Geometric details like the tight rows of lights, un-adorned windows, and the black lacquered door frame bring order to the apartment, while empty planes act as a canvas for the client's outstanding collection of American art and African sculpture.

Diese entkernte Wohnung der Jahrhundertwende, eher desorganisiert als offen, wurde den Händen des Teams PKSB anvertraut. Die Architekten wollten einen formalen Eingang und eine logische Struktur heraufbeschwören, ohne jedoch zum status quo zurückzukehren. Ein elliptisches Foyer wurde eingebaut und ein Flur wiederhergestellt: durch eine Reihe freigelegter tragender Säulen und einen 10,5 Meter langen, metallenen Baldachin sowie Strahlern, die Decke und schwarz getönte Böden beleuchten. Geometrische Details wie die Lampenreihen, undekorierte Fenster und der schwarzlackierte Türrahmen bringen Ordnung in das Apartment, während leere Flächen als Hintergrund für eine Skulpturen- und Kunst-Sammlung dienen.

Cet appartement dépouillé du début du siècle, plus désorganisé que diaphane, a été placé entre les mains de l'équipe PKSB. Les architectes ont souhaité rendre la sensation d'une entrée formelle et d'une structure logique, sans revenir à l'original. Une réception elliptique a été créée, et un couloir restauré grâce à une série de colonnes structurelles nues, et à un dais métallique suspendu de 10,5 mètres. Des spots illuminent le plafond et les parquets en ébène teintée. Les détails géométriques, tels des rangées de lumières, des fenêtres simples et le châssis de porte laqué ordonnent l'appartement, des plans vides servant de toile pour l'exceptionnelle collection d'art américain et de sculptures africaines du client.

This apartment boasts an extensive art collection
amidst an extravagant setting of eclectic furniture.
The office is placed inside a free-standing
structure that divides the living room from the bedroom.

Dieses Apartment zeichnet sich durch eine umfangreiche Kunstsammlung
inmitten einer extravaganten Szenerie ausgesuchter Möbel aus. Das
Arbeitszimmer wurde in einem freistehendem Element untergebracht,
das den Wohnraum vom Schlafzimmer trennt.

Cet appartement se flatte d'un collection artistique étendue, dans un
cadre extravagant au mobilier éclectique. Le bureau est situé au sein
d'une structure sans appui, séparant le séjour de la chambre.

Wall Street Loft

Chroma AD

Photos: © David M. Joseph
Completion date: 1999
chroma@thing.net

This bustling business area is characterized by skyscrapers along narrow streets, making light a primary concern for the construction of this apartment. In order to capture scattered rays of sunshine and light reflected off other buildings, the architects took full advantage of the numerous windows, 11-foot ceilings, and highly reflective floors. The elements consume all available daylight and bounce it across the black and white interior. Exposed concrete beams and columns, along with translucent sliding doors and fabrics, divide the areas and create a spacious environment. These ample and luminous light boxes provide a welcome change of scenery against the city's cluttered urban landscape.

Im turbulenten Geschäftsviertel der Wall Street, wo Wolkenkratzer schmale Straßen säumen, ist das Licht von großer Wichtigkeit. Um vereinzelte Sonnenstrahlen und das von anderen Gebäuden reflektierte Licht aufzufangen, nutzten die Architekten zahlreiche Fenster, die 3,30 Meter hohen Decken und die stark spiegelnden Böden. Diese Elemente absorbieren das verfügbare Tageslicht und reflektieren es auf die schwarzweiße Einrichtung. Sichtbare Betonträger und –pfeiler sowie durchscheinende Schiebetüren und Wandschirme aus Tuch trennen einzelne Bereiche voneinander und schaffen eine geräumige, gemütliche Atmosphäre. Die weiten, hellen Lichtkästen sind eine willkommene Abwechslung in der vollgestopften urbanen Landschaft.

Wall Street, quartier d'affaires animé, caractérisé par ses gratte-ciel et ses rues étroites, a fait de la lumière l'enjeu principal de la construction de cet appartement. Pour saisir les rares rayons de soleil et la lumière reflétée par d'autres immeubles, les architectes ont pleinement tiré parti des multiples fenêtres, des hauts plafonds et des sols réfléchissants. Ces éléments absorbent tout la lumière et la font rejaillir au travers de l'intérieur noir et blanc. Piliers et poutres apparents en béton, fenêtres coulissantes et châssis translucides, divisent les aires et créent un environnement spacieux et intime. Ces boîtes à lumière, amples et lumineuses, apportent un changement de décor bienvenu dans le paysage urbain encombré.

Ost/Kuttner Apartment

Kolatan MacDonald

Photos: © Michael Moran
Completion date: 2000

The architect designed this flat using an arbitrary system of 'sites'. A web of sites was computed in which profiles of everyday domestic objects were cross-referenced through a computer. The unpredictable results yielded topographies with an unconventional layout and distribution of areas. There is no clear distribution in this apartment and rooms flow into one another in unusual and unexpected ways. The bed and bathroom, for example, is one single unit that forms a continuous, seamless surface. Wood, steel, velvet, and reflective plastic-like surfaces come in assorted bold colors. This design method is as unorthodox as the variety of materials and colors used within the entire space.

Der Architekt entwarf diese Wohnung, indem er ein willkürliches Aufstellungssystem benutzte. Im Computer wurde ein Koordinatennetz angelegt, in dem die Umrisse alltäglicher Haushaltsgegenstände vom Computer selbständig angeordnet wurden. Die unvorhersehbaren Ergebnisse brachten Topographien mit unkonventionellem Layout und Raumordnung hervor. Es gibt in diesem Apartment keine klare Aufteilung und die Räume fließen auf ungewöhnliche Weise ineinander. Das Bett/Bad beispielsweise ist eine Einheit, die eine nahtlose Oberfläche bildet. Die Methode des Entwurfes ist genauso unorthodox wie die Vielfalt der Materialien und Farbschemata, die in diesem Raum zum Einsatz kamen.

L'architecte a conçu cet appartement avec un système arbitraire de «sites». Un réseau de sites a été calculé en combinant par ordinateur les profils d'unités domestiques quotidiennes. Le résultat, imprévisible, a produit des topographies dotées de disposition et distribution des aires peu conventionnelles. Il n'y a pas d'organisation claire dans ce lieu, les pièces glissant les unes dans les autres de façon inhabituelle. Ainsi, le lit/bain constitue une unité simple, formant une surface continue et sans raccords. La méthode de conception est peu orthodoxe, de même que la diversité de matériaux et les combinaisons de couleurs employés.

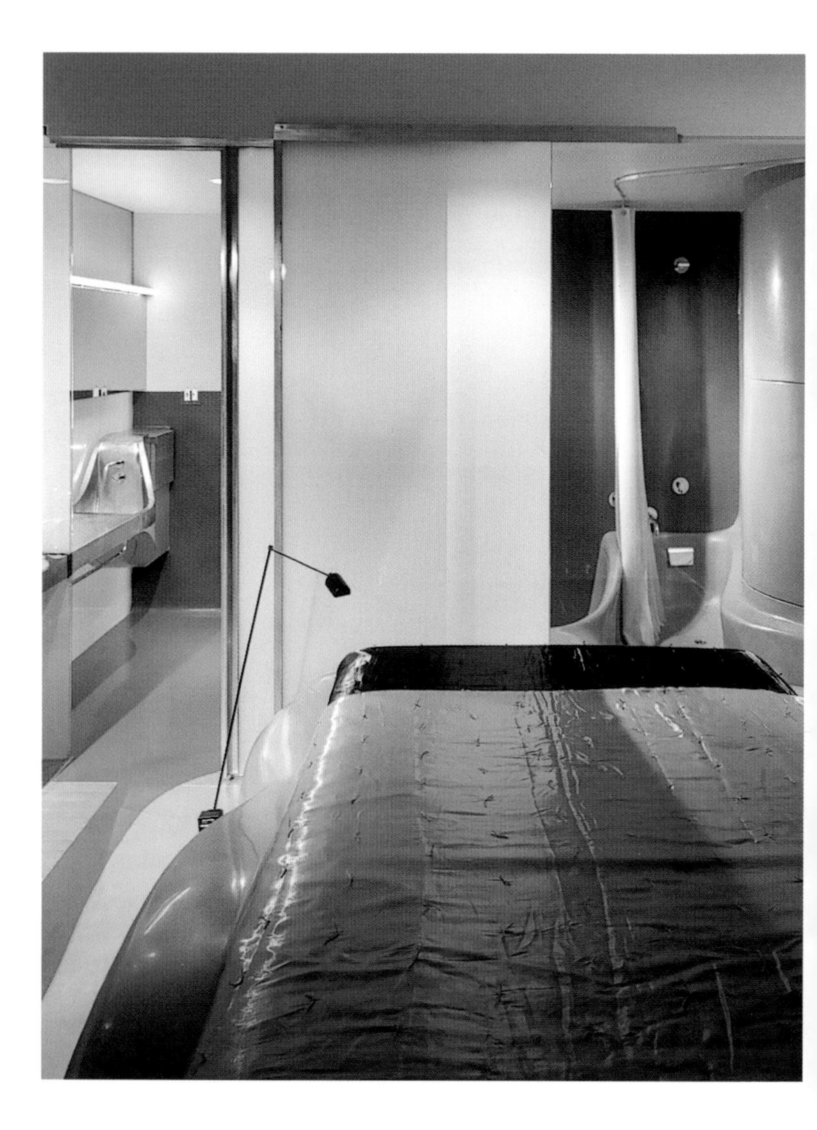

2+1 Apartment

Robert D. Henry

Photos: © Paul Warchol, © Dan Bibb
Completion date: 1999

The design scheme envisioned by this apartment's architect and owner Robert Henry creates a light, open, and free-flowing space that accommodates his son's activities without sacrificing his and his wife's high aesthetic standards. The 20-foot high ceiling permitted different levels for the living area, kitchen, and bedrooms. A dramatic 13 ft high window saturates the home with natural light. Distinguishing elements include the cantilevered bent steel lounge that hovers over the lower level, the surfboard-shaped drifwood breakfast table, and the built-in floor playpen and toy storage area that transforms into an adult space thanks to a custom tea table that hinges down from the wall.

Der vom Eigentümer, dem Architekten Robert Henry, entwickelte Entwurf schuf einen hellen, offenen und fließenden Raum, der der Lebhaftigkeit seines Sohnes gewachsen ist, ohne die ästhetischen Standards der Eltern zu verraten. Dank der 6 Meter hohen Decke liegen Wohnraum, Küche und Schlafzimmer auf verschiedenen Ebenen. Viel Stauraum hält die Flächen frei, und ein 4 Meter hohes Fenster überströmt das Apartment mit Tageslicht. Eine an Stahlträgern aufgehängte Liege schwebt über der oberen Ebene; der Frühstückstisch aus Treibholz hat die Form eines Surfbretts und der im Boden eingebaute Laufstall kann dank eines ausklappbaren Beistelltischs für Erwachsene umgewandelt werden.

Le plan conceptuel imaginé par Robert Henry, architecte et propriétaire de cet appartement, crée un espace lumineux, ouvert et fluide qui accueille les activités de son fils sans sacrifier les exigences esthétiques de son couple. Un plafond à 6 mètres autorise différents niveaux pour le séjour, la cuisine et les chambres. L'espace reste dégagé grâce aux nombreux rangements, une sensationnelle fenêtre de 4 mètres saturant la maison de lumière naturelle. Les éléments distinctifs comprennent un sofa en porte-à-faux en acier recourbé, planant au-dessus du premier niveau, une table en bois flotté en forme de surf, et un espace pour enfant, avec un parc et un coffre à jouets encastrés dans le sol, devenant une zo-ne adulte grâce à une table à thé s'abaissant depuis le mur.

LUCIAN FREUD

John Derian Apartment

John Derian

Photos: © Dan Bibb
Completion date: 2000

Home to a passionate collector of others´ craftsmanship, this three-room apartment features pieces from his own interior design shop like handmade tableware, colorful antiques, and flea market finds. The space reflects the owner' s romantic sensibility. In a style far more rural baroque than urban minimalist, this home offers a change of scenery with its warm and homey interiors. Luscious flowers, mixed patterns, and abundant handcrafted elements fill the house, creating a cheerful, lived-in atmosphere. Worn out antique mirrors and armchairs set against aged dark wood and cream walls give the space the charm and character of a rural home inside one of the most urban and contemporary cities of the world.

Hier wohnt ein passionierter Sammler. Zu diesem Drei-Zimmer-Apartment gehören kunstgewerbliche Objekte genauso wie Stücke aus dem Design-Shop des Besitzes. Der Raum spiegelt die romantische Sensibilität des Eigentümers wider. Eher im ländlichen Barockstil als städtischem Minimalismus gehalten, bietet diese Wohnung mit ihrer warmen und heimeligen Einrichtung einen wahren Szenenwechsel. Üppige Blumen, Mustermix und Kunstgewerbe füllen das Haus und schaffen eine heitere, wohnliche Atmosphäre. Antike Spiegel und Sessel setzen sich von altem, dunklen Holz ab, und cremefarbene Wände verleihen dem Raum Charme und den Eindruck eines ländlichen Zuhauses mitten in einer der modernsten städtischen Metropolen der Welt.

Foyer d'un collectionneur passionné, ce trois pièces accueille des pièces artisanales, ainsi que des objets provenant de sa boutique de design, comme de la vaisselle faite à la main, des antiquités pittoresques et des trouvailles chinées. Le lieu reflète l'âme romantique du propriétaire. Préférant le baroque rural au minimalisme urbain, la maison offre un changement de décor avec ses intérieurs chaleureux et intimes. Fleurs sensuelles, motifs variés, éléments d'artisanat abondants remplissent la demeure, créant une atmosphère gaie et vivante. Fauteuils et miroirs anciens fatigués résonnent avec les murs crèmes et les bois sombres vieillis, donnant à l'espace le charme et la personnalité d'un foyer rural, au cœur d'une des cités les plus urbanisées et modernes du monde.

Levy Loft

Ali Tayar

Photos: © John Hall
Completion date: 1993
mtayar@rcn.com

This loft functions primarily through the use of a transformable panel system. Designed around a tightly defined core that contains the kitchen, guest bathroom and laundry room, a fixed half-height room divider and two sliding, ceiling-mounted, full-length room dividers define the den and guest room areas. Extended deployable walls provide privacy in the study that doubles as a guest room. A two-foot deep wood sill structure was inserted to encase the steel-framed grid of the loft's industrial windows. The presence of cherrywood, cork flooring and colorful decorative details add warmth and intimacy to this glass enclosed space with views of the urban landscape.

Dieser Loft funktioniert in erster Linie durch den Einsatz eines wandelbaren Systems aus Paneelen. Es wurde um einen eng abgegrenzten Kern herum entworfen, der Küche, Gästebadezimmer und eine Waschkammer enthält, wobei ein fixierter Raumteiler sowie zwei bewegliche, in der Decke befestigte, raumhohe Faltelemente das Arbeitszimmer und den Bereich des Gästezimmes definieren. Verlängerte Aufstellwände sorgen für Intimsphäre in diesem Teil des Lofts. Ein 60 Zentimeter tiefer hölzerner Sims wurde eingebaut, um das stahlgerahmte Raster der industriellen Fenster des Lofts zu verkleiden. Kirschholz, Korkböden und bunte Details verleihen diesem glasgerahmten Raum mit Blick auf die urbane Landschaft Wärme und Intimität.

Ce loft fonctionne essentiellement au moyen d'un système de panneaux modulable. Le lieu est conçu au-tour d'un noyau strictement défini, contenant la cuisine, la salle de bain invité, et la buanderie. Une cloison fixe à mi-hauteur et deux autres coulissantes à pleine hauteur, suspendues au plafond, distinguent bureau et chambre d'hôte. De grands murs dépliables offrent l'intimité à l'étude/chambre d'hôte. Un rebord en bois, profond de 60 cm, a été ajouté pour accueillir le grillage encadré d'acier des fenêtres industrielles du loft. Cerisier, sol de liège et détails pittoresques ajoutent chaleur et intimité à cet espace cerné de verre, avec vue sur le paysage urbain.

KAY

K-Loft

George Ranalli

Photos: © Paul Warchol
Completion date: 1996

The main challenge in renovating this space was the lack of natural light, since there are windows only in the front and rear. The architect solved the problem by introducing a series of volumes that leave the openings unobstructed and that maintain space in between each other so that the available light can flow straight through. The form of wooden panels used for these constructions was altered, and their edges were carved out geometrically to change their profile and perspective of scale. In order to retain the spirit of the original structure and to contrast with the high finish of the new materials, the expansive rough brick walls were left exposed.

Die größte Herausforderung bei der Renovierung lag im Mangel an natürlichem Licht, da Fenster nur an den Stirnseiten vorhanden waren. Der Architekt löste das Problem durch den Einbau mehrerer Körper, welche die Öffnungen unverstellt lassen und Abstand voneinander bewahren, so dass das Licht ungehindert durch das Apartment fluten kann. Die Form der Holzpaneele wurde für ihren Bau verändert: die Ecken wurden geometrisch ausgeschnitten, um Profil und Maßstab zu verändern. Um den Geist der ursprünglichen Konstruktion zu erhalten und mit den hochwertigen Finishs der neuen Materialien zu kontrastieren, blieb das raue Ziegelmauerwerk sichtbar.

L'absence de lumière naturelle a constitué le principal défi de cette rénovation, les fenêtres ne perçant que la façade et l'arrière de l'espace. L'architecte a résolu la question en introduisant une série de volumes, laissant les ouvertures dégagées et maintenant une distance entre eux afin que la lumière puisse affluer librement. La forme des panneaux de bois utilisés pour ces contructions a été modifiée, leurs bords taillés géométriquement pour changer leur profil et leur échelle de perspective. Afin de conserver l'esprit originel de la structure, les larges murs en brique brute sont restés apparents contrastant avec la haute finition des nouveaux matériaux.

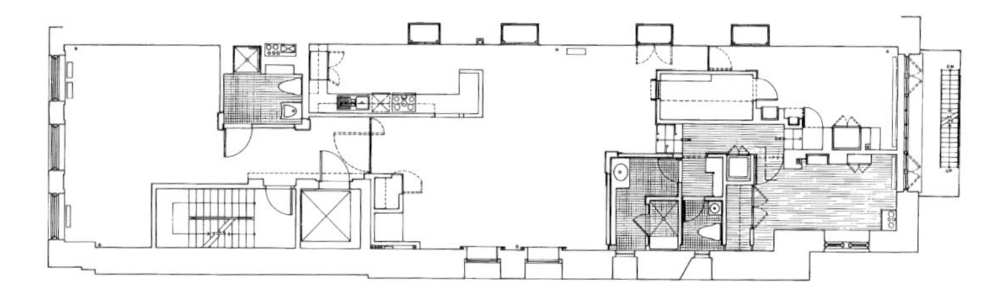

Kaufman Berger Residence

David Spiker

Photos: © Michael Moran
Completion date: 1998

Redesigning this apartment involved one single architectural intervention; an oblique line drawn from the entry to the window wall. A traditional New York entry hall provides access to several rooms, a playroom, and a gallery. The office wall is a compound curve finished in tinted plaster to contrast with the rest of the living spaces. The removing of old office ceilings revealed an abstract framework of beams, and the new ceiling was used to supply storage and furniture that holds the clients´ vast collection of polychromatic cultural artifacts. The bathroom is finished in tiny pale green glass tiles. Colorful walls and curious objects are the most notable features of this delicious apartment.

Zur Umgestaltung dieses Apartments genügte eine einzige architektonische Geste: eine schräge, vom Eingang bis zur Fensterfront gezogene Linie. Eine klassische New Yorker Eingangshalle erschließt mehrere Räume, ein Spielzimmer und eine Galerie. Die Wand des Büros ist eine zusammengesetzte, in farbigem Putz ausgeführte Kurve, die mit dem übrigen Wohnraum kontrastiert. Durch die Entfernung der Decke im Büroraum legte der Architekt ein abstraktes Balken-Flechtwerk frei. Die neue Decke nimmt Leitungen und Möbel auf, in denen eine umfangreiche Kunstsammlung polychromer Artefakte aufbewahrt wird. Das Badezimmer ist mit mattgrünen Glasfliesen gekachelt. Bemerkenswert sind auch die bunten Wände und Kuriosa.

Le remodelage de cet appartement a requis une seule intervention architecturale: une oblique tracée de l'entrée jusqu'au mur vitré. Un hall d'entrée new-yorkais traditionnel offre un accès à plusieurs pièces, une salle de jeu et une galerie. Le mur du bureau est une courbe complexe, se terminant en plâtre teinté contrastant avec les autres espaces de séjour. En retirant les plafonds de l'ancien bureau, l'architecte a mis à nu une ossature abstraite de poutres. Le nouveau plafond loge accessoires et mobilier, contenant la vaste collection d'objets d'art traditionnels polychromes du client. Le fini de la salle de bain est rendu par de petits carreaux vert pâle. Murs colorés et objets originaux sont les autres éléments notables de ce délicieux appartement.

THE ILIAD OF HOMER
JEWISH POETRY

Books sit on shelves and ethnic masks rest on walls. A fold down bed transforms the study into a guest bedroom. In the kitchen, a window reveals a framed view of the World Trade Center. The loft combines traditional moldings within an abstract framework of walls and beams.

Bücher füllen die Regale und Masken hängen an den Wänden, ein Klappbett verwandelt den Arbeitsraum in ein Gästezimmer. In der Küche enthüllt ein Fenster den gerahmten Blick auf das World Trade Center. Das Loft kombiniert klassische Deckenfriese mit abstraktem Fachwerk aus Wänden und Balken.

Livres sur rayonnages, masques ethniques aux murs. Un lit pliant transforme l'étude en chambre d'hôte. Dans la cuisine, une fenêtre révèle une vue encadrée du World Trade Center. Le loft associe moulures traditionnelles et ossature abstraite de murs et de poutres.

Industrial Loft

Alexander Jiménez

Photos: © Jordi Miralles
Completion date: 1998

The outstanding features of this loft lie in the simplicity with which its functional requirements were carried out. Although the existing wood floors were damaged and thus replaced, the house maintains its industrial aspects, including the restored brick walls and wooden ceiling beams. Partitions were erected to enclose the bedroom and bathroom. The kitchen opens up to the rest of the house, but is visually separated by rugs underneath the furniture. The frame of the structure containing the kitchen intersects with the lateral walls and leaves a gap underneath the ceiling for practical storage space. Abundant light flows throughout the open space, accentuating the loft's comfortable and homey interiors.

Die Besonderheiten dieses Lofts liegen in der Einfachheit, mit der die funktionalen Bedürfnisse ausgeführt wurden. Obwohl der schadhafte Dielenboden ausgewechselt werden musste, bewahrt das Apartment durch das sanierte Mauerwerk und die Holzbalken seinen industriellen Look. Trennwände wurden eingezogen, um Bad und Schlafzimmer zu verschließen. Die Küche liegt offen, ist jedoch durch ausgelegte Teppiche optisch abgetrennt. Der Rahmen, der die Küche aufnimmt, überschneidet sich mit den Seitenwänden und lässt unter der Decke praktischen Stauraum frei. Verschwenderisch scheint das Licht durch den ganzen Raum und akzentuiert die heimelige Einrichtung.

L'aspect remarquable de ce loft tient à la simplicité avec laquelle il a été pourvu à ses besoins fonctionnels. Bien que les parquets existants, endommagés, aient du être remplacés, la maison conserve son apparence industrielle, incluant les murs de briques restaurés et les poutres en bois. Des cloisons ont été dressées, ceignant chambre et salle de bain, et la cuisine s'ouvre sur le reste de la maison tout en restant séparée visuellement par des tapis placés sous le mobilier. Le cadre de la structure contenant la cuisine se croise avec les murs latéraux, créant un espace de rangement pratique sous le plafond. Une lumière généreuse afflue par l'espace ouvert, accentuant l'aspect accueillant et confortable de ce loft.

SONY

The Rosenberg Residence

Belmont Freeman Architects

Photos: © Christopher Wesnofske
Completion date: 1998
e.nicol@belmontfreeman.com

This loft is divided equally into two levels that serve as an office, studio, and home for its art-loving resident. The upper floor contains a living room, kitchen and two bedrooms, and its partitions are disconnected from the exterior, drowning the space with daylight. Two mobile screens, one of plasterboard and the other of translucent glass, make distribution flexible. The lower level, vertically linked by an industrial-like ladder, has a restored sandblasted concrete floor covered in zinc casting and functions as an office and studio. The materials used, including concrete, maple, stainless steel, and laminated glass, offer a contemporary elegance magnified by the owner's outstanding collection of modern furniture.

Der Loft ist in zwei gleichgroße Ebenen unterteilt und dient als Büro, Studio und Wohnung eines Kunstliebhabers. Die obere Etage nehmen Wohnzimmer, Küche und zwei Schlafzimmer ein. Da die Raumteiler nicht bis an die Außenwand reichen, durchflutet Tageslicht die ganze Ebene. Zwei bewegliche Wandschirme, aus Gipskarton bzw. Glas, machen die Aufteilung flexibel. Die untere Ebene, vertikal durch eine industrieartige Leiter erschlossen, hat einen sandgestrahlten Betonboden mit einer Zinkbeschichtung und fungiert als Büro und Studio. Die eingesetzten Materialien, darunter Beton, Ahorn, Edelstahl und Schichtglas sorgen für eine aktuelle Eleganz, die durch die einzigartige Sammlung moderner Möbel des Eigentümers bereichert wird.

Ce loft est divisé en deux niveaux égaux tenant lieu de bureau, d'atelier et de foyer pour ses occupants, amateurs d'art. L'étage supérieur contient un séjour, une cuisine et deux chambres, ses cloisons déconnectées de l'extérieur inondant l'espace de lumière naturelle. Deux écrans mobiles, l'un en placoplâtre et l'autre en verre translucide, offrent une répartition flexible. Le niveau inférieur, relié verticalement par une échelle de type industriel, dispose d'un sol en béton sablé et recouvert de zinc, et sert de bureau et d'atelier. Les matériaux utilisés, béton, érable, acier inox et verre feuilleté, offrent une élégance contemporaine magnifiée par la remarquable collection de meubles modernes du propriétaire.

Greenberg Loft

Smith-Miller & Hawkinson Architects

Photos: © Matteo Piazza
Completion date: 1997
dimcheff@smharch.com

Architects created a dyadic space that functions as both a dwelling and as an exhibition area for its owner, an art collector from New York. The lower floor of the duplex contains most of the rooms, and the upper floor accommodates two sub-levels that were built to take advantage of the available space provided by the high ceilings. Sliding wood-veneer doors, large inclined motorized windows, suspended spotlights, and a monochrome palette allow for interconnecting spaces, plenty of natural light, and a sense of weightlessness and calm. This spectacular loft serves as the perfect setting for its owner's art collection and is a peaceful refuge from the hectic city.

Die Architekten gestalteten einen Zwillingsraum, der sowohl als Wohnung als auch als Ausstellungsfläche für den Besitzer, einen Kunstsammler, dient. Die meisten Räume befinden sich im unteren der beiden Geschosse; auf der oberen Ebene wurden zwei Zwischengeschosse eingezogen, um die hohe Decke auszunutzen. Schiebetüren aus Furnierholz, große motorgesteuerte Dachfenster, aufgehängte Strahler und monochrome Farben sorgen für zusammenhängende Räume, reichliches Tageslicht und den Eindruck von Leichtigkeit und Ruhe. Der spektakuläre Loft ist der perfekte Rahmen für die Kunstsammlung und eine friedliche Oase angesichts der hektischen Stadt.

Les architectes ont crée un espace dual, tenant lieu de résidence et de salle d'exposition pour son propriétaire, un collectionneur new-yorkais. Le niveau inférieur du duplex accueille la majeure partie des pièces, l'étage recevant deux sous-niveaux créés pour tirer parti de l'espace disponible offert par le haut plafond. Portes coulissantes plaquées en bois, grandes fenêtres inclinées et motorisées, spots suspendus et palette monochrome facilitent la communication entre les espaces, l'afflux de lumière naturelle et une sensation d'apesanteur, et de calme. Ce loft spectaculaire est le décor parfait pour la collection d'art du propriétaire, et un havre de paix loin de la frénésie de la ville.

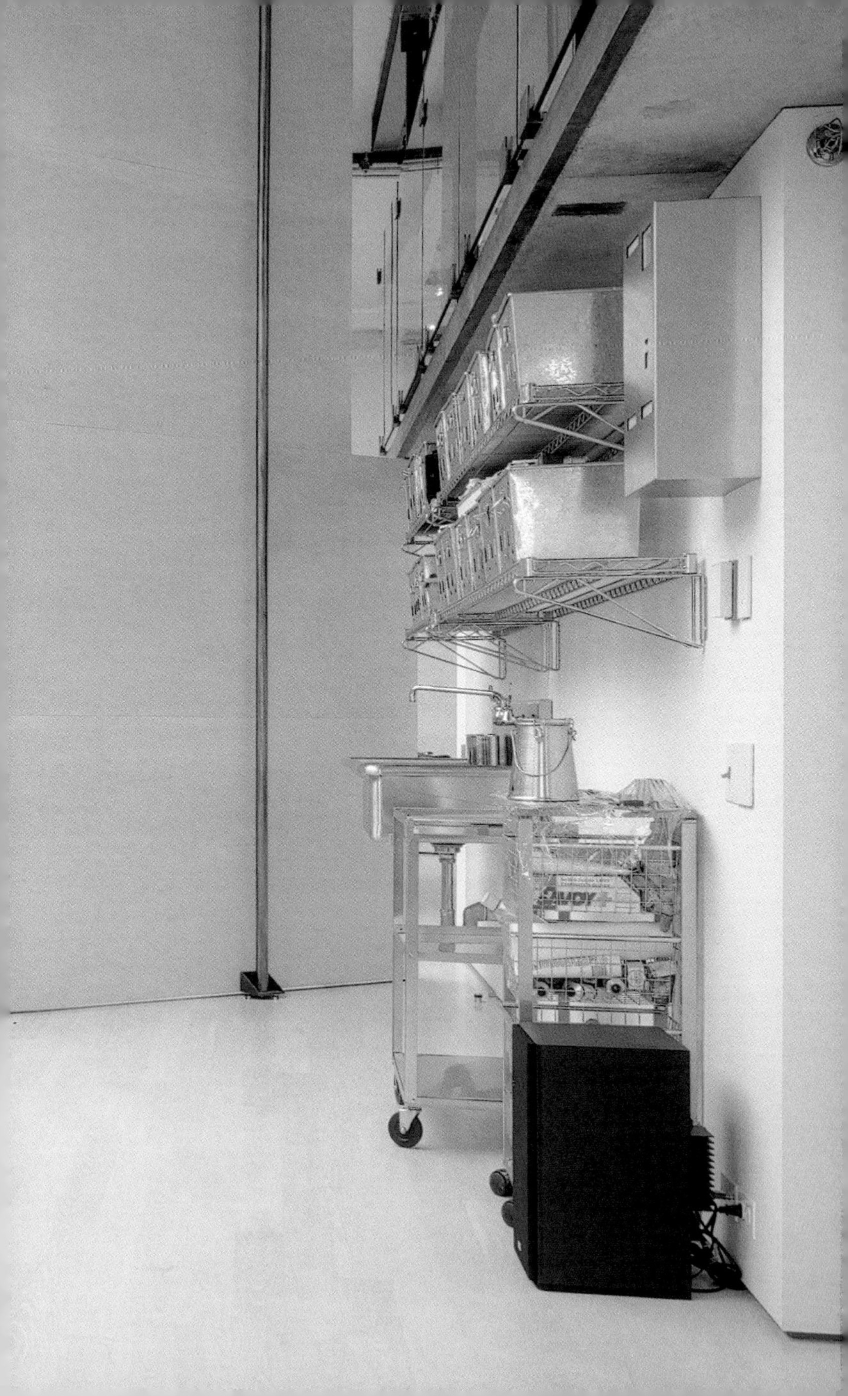

Pekarsky Residence

Cho Slade

Photos: © Jordi Miralles
Completion date: 1999

Massive 20 cm thick exposed brick walls enclose and extend the full depth of the apartment. The central core contains the kitchen, study, and master bathroom, around which the dining area, living room and master bedroom revolve. To contrast the heavy stationary brick walls, translucent materials were used to contstruct the ceiling, walls, and doors, revealing the shadows of internal pipes and mechanical equipment. The space is cleverly organised using multi-purpose features: A large sliding pantry opens to enclose the study, sliding black and white photographs conceal a cloakroom, and in the bedroom the walk-in closet doubles as a headboard with built in reading lights and night table.

Massive, 50 Zentimeter dicke Sichtziegelmauern umschließen das Apartment. Ein Kern enthält Küche, Studio und Badezimmer; um ihn herum gruppieren sich der Essbereich, das Wohnzimmer und das Schlafzimmer. Als Kontrast zu den schweren, tragenden Ziegelwänden setzte der Architekt für Decken, Trennwände und Türen lichtdurchlässige Materialien ein, so dass die Silhouetten der Rohrleitungen und Haustechnik durchschimmern. Der Raum ist intelligent aufgeteilt. Eine große mobile Speisekammer öffnet sich, um das Arbeitszimmer abzugrenzen; Schwarz-Weiß-Fotos an Laufschienen verbergen eine Garderobe und ein begehbarer Kleiderschrank im Schlafzimmer dient gleichzeitig als Kopfende mit eingebauten Lampen und Nachttischen.

De massifs murs de 50 cm, aux briques apparentes, closent l'appartement et étendent sa profondeur. Au cœur se trouvent la cuisine, l'étude et la salle de bain principale, autours desquelles gravitent salle à manger, séjour et chambre principale. En contraste aux imposants murs de briques, l'architecte a employé des matériaux translucides pour confectionner plafonds, murs et portes, révélant les ombres de la tuyauterie et des équipements techniques. L'espace est astucieusement distribué, recourant à des éléments multifonctions. Un grand cellier glissoir s'ouvre pour clore l'étude, des photos blanc et noir coulissantes escamotent un vestiaire, et le dressing dans la chambre est aussi une tête de lit dotée de chevets et de liseuses encastrées.

MILK

The sliding pantry door opens to close off the office. The arched doorways demonstrate the thickness of the massive brick walls.

Das Schieberegal der Vorratskammer öffnet sich und verschließt das Arbeitszimmer. Die Bögen der Flurdurchgänge zeigen die Stärke der massiven Ziegelmauern an.

La porte coulissante de l'office permet de clore le bureau. Les ouvertures voûtées soulignent l'épaisseur des murs de brique massifs.

Ponikvar Penthouse

Hariri & Hariri

Photos: © Paul Warchol
Completion date: 1999

This penthouse was designed for a bachelor attorney who loves and collects books. Inspired by the grandiose scenery from the 1,000-square foot wraparound terrace overlooking the Hudson River and the Empire State Building, the area was treated almost as an archaeological site. Elements like old water and waste pipes were uncovered, cleaned and displayed inside a glass showcase that separates the living room from the dining room. A staircase supported by the wall emerges from the limestone floors below, leading up to the bedroom and library, which are divided by pivoting bookshelves. The bulky furniture, ceiling beams, and spectacular surroundings balance the space's luminous and airy quality.

Dieses Penthouse wurde für einen Anwalt und Bücher-Sammler renoviert. Inspiriert von der grandiosen Szenerie, die sich vor der 90 m^2 großen umlaufenden Terrasse mit Blick auf den Hudson, Washington Square und das Empire State Building ausbreitet, wurde der Raum fast wie eine archäologische Fundstätte behandelt. Alte Wasser- und Abfallrohre wurden freigelegt, gesäubert und in einem Glaskasten ausgestellt, die den Wohnraum vom Esszimmer trennt. In die Wand eingelassene Treppenstufen gehen aus dem Kalksteinboden hervor und führen ins Schlafzimmer und in die Bibliothek. Voluminöse Möbel, Deckenbalken und die spektakuläre Umgebung bilden ein Gegengewicht zur Helligkeit und Luftigkeit des Raumes.

Ce penthouse a été remodelé pour un avocat célibataire, amateur et collectionneur de livres. Enflammé par le décor grandiose de la terrasse de 90 m^2 qui le ceint, donnant sur l'Hudson, Washington Square et l'Empire State Building, l'espace a été traité quasiment comme un site archéologique. La tuyauterie a été mise à jour, décapée et exposée dans une vitrine de verre, séparant le séjour de la salle à manger. Un escalier dans le mur émerge du sol en comblanchien, menant à la chambre et à la bibliothèque, séparées l'une de l'autre par des étagères pivotantes. Mobilier opulent, poutres au plafond et cadre spectaculaire équilibrent la nature claire et lumineuse de l'espace.

Bachelor Pad

Ed Mills & Associates

Photos: © Chuck Choi
Completion date: 1998

Three one-bedroom flats were joined into one single apartment on the top two floors of an Art Deco tower in Greenwich Village. A cantilevered staircase made of wood and steel leads to a large skylight fitted with a cylindrical steel structure that spills light onto the office desk. Downstairs, an plaster wall displays dramatically lit works of art. A stainless steel and glass wall opens up the living room for parties or subdivides it for greater intimacy. Both levels have access to extensive terraces. The space was designed to display and complement the owner's important art and furniture collection. The result is an eclectic and modern space with functional attributes and aesthetic appeal.

Drei Zwei-Zimmer-Apartments der beiden obersten Etagn eines Art Déco-Wolkenkratzers in Greenwich Village wurden zu einer Wohnung zusammengeschlossen. Eine neue freitragende Treppe aus Holz und Stahl hat ein rundes Oberlicht; an ihrer Seitenwand aus künstlerischem Gipsputz werden theatralisch beleuchtete Kunstwerke ausgestellt. Eine Wand aus Edelstahl und Glas öffnet das Wohnzimmer für Partys oder unterteilt es für eine intimere Privatsphäre. Beide Ebenen haben Zugang zu großzügigen Terrassen. Dieses moderne Zuhause wurde für die Ausstellung der bedeutenden Kunst- und Möbelsammlung gestaltet. Das Ergebnis ist ein exquisiter Raum mit funktionellen Attributen und einer ästhetischen Ausstrahlung.

Trois appartements d'une chambre ont été réunis en un seul, sur les deux derniers étages d'une tour Art déco de Greenwich Village. Un nouvel escalier suspendu, en bois et acier, met en évidence de grandes lucarnes et un mur de plâtre orné d'œuvres d'art éclairées théâtralement. Un mur de verre et d'acier ouvre le séjour pour recevoir, ou le subdivise pour plus d'intimité. Chaque niveau accède aux vastes terrasses. Ce foyer moderne a été conçu pour mettre en valeur et compléter l'importante collection artistique et de mobilier du propriétaire. Est né un espace moderne, éclectique, fonctionnel et doté d'un charme esthétique.

Picasso and Braque
PIONEERING CUBISM
Picasso and Braque: Pioneering Cubism
THE EPIC OF LIFE

Kastan Residence

Chapman & Chapman

Photos: © Björg
Completion date: 1999
wid@chapmanarch.com

Once a parking garage, this loft was renovated and designed for an advisor of 19th and 20th century fine art photography. The space serves as ample and intimate living quarters with an area reserved for a gallery to display the owner's photography collection. Laid out on four levels, the home contains a skylit office space and master bedroom, dining and living rooms, a den that doubles as a guestroom, and two baths, topped off by 1,600-square feet of terraced roof space. Interesting elements include the 40-foot long plaster bar that acts as a photo hanging gallery, the framed views of the steel staircase from the dining room, and the tatami bed with inset tatami mats in the master bedroom.

Dieser Loft war früher eine Garage und wurde für einen Sachverständigen für Fotokunst umgestaltet. Der Raum dient als weitläufige private Wohnfläche mit einem Bereich auf der Galerie, der für die Ausstellung der Fotografien-Sammlung des Besitzers reserviert ist. Zu dieser sich über vier Ebenen erstreckenden Wohnung gehören ein über Dachfenster erhelltes Büro sowie Schlafzimmer, Wohn- und Esszimmer, ein wandelbares Arbeits-/Gästezimmer und zwei Bäder; das ganze wird von einer 150 m^2 großen Dachterrasse vollendet. Interessant sind das 12 Meter lange verputzte Schrankelement, das als Fotogalerie dient, die gerahmten Blicke auf die Stahltreppe vom Esszimmer aus und das Bett auf einem Podest mit eingelassenen Tatami-Matten.

Autrefois un garage, ce loft a été rénové et conçu pour un consultant en photo d'art XIXe et XXe. L'espace est un cadre de vie vaste et intime, une partie étant réservée pour une galerie présentant la collection de photographies du propriétaire. Sur quatre niveaux, le foyer accueille un espace bureau avec lucarne, une chambre principale, salon et salle à manger, une étude/chambre d'hôte convertible et deux salles de bain, tous couronnés par une terrasse de 150 m2 sur le toit. Les éléments saisissants comprennent un bar en plâtre de 12 mètres servant de lieu d'accrochage pour photos, les vues encadrées de l'escalier d'acier depuis la salle à manger, et le lit de la chambre principale, doté de tatamis.

Home to a psychiatrist and photography dealer, books and photographs are crucial elements that influenced the overall design.

Bücher und Fotos sind in diesem Zuhause eines Psychiaters und Foto-Händlers entscheidend und haben die gesamte Einrichtung beeinflusst.

Pour le foyer d'un psychiatre et d'un marchand de photos, livres et photographies sont des éléments essentiels qui influencent le design d'ensemble.

Private Residence

Dean/Wolf Architects

Photos: © Dean/Wolf Architects
Completion date: 1997

Architects redesigned this loft to allow natural light to filter through to the back of the house. The irregular shape of the space created two very dark small rooms which were consequently torn down and opened up to the rest of the space to form one diaphanous area. Both living and working areas overlap through the implementation of mobile components that create interconnecting spaces. Dual structures form the primary components of the home: the office sits next to the dining room, and the bathroom, enclosed by a curved wall, is flanked by a staircase. The bedroom and table is another dual structure. Furniture has a minimalist tendency, maintaining the interiors light and uncluttered.

Die Architekten gestalteten diesen Loft um, damit natürliches Licht bis in den hinteren Teil des Hauses dringen konnte. Auf Grund des unregelmäßigen Zuschnitts der Wohnung bestanden zwei dunkle kleine Zimmer, die entfernt und zum übrigen Raum geöffnet wurden, um einen einzigen offenen Bereich zu bilden. Wohn- und Arbeitsbereiche überlappen sich dank mobiler Komponenten und der Verkettung der Räume. Das Büro liegt neben dem Esszimmer und ist optisch durch eine geschwungene Wand abgeteilt, die das Bad umschließt, das wiederum durch die angrenzende Treppe abgesteckt wird. Die Einrichtung tendiert zum Minimalismus und lässt die Räume leicht und frei.

Les architectes ont remodelé ce loft, pour que la lumière naturelle s'infiltre vers le fond de la maison. L'asymétrie de ce volume créait deux petites pièces sombres, logiquement supprimées pour s'ouvrir et former un seul espace diaphane. Les aires de séjour et de travail se superposent au moyen de composants mobiles et d'espaces s'interconnectant. Bureau et salle à manger sont côte à côte, séparés visuellement par un mur curviligne qui ceignait la salle de bain, définie à son tour par l'escalier la jouxtant. La tendance minimaliste du mobilier préserve les intérieurs clairs et dégagés.

Renaud Residence

Cha & Innerhofer

Photos: © Dao-Lou Zha
Completion date: 1998

Home to a young banker, this Soho loft is a peaceful retreat from the everyday hubbub of the city. Light wood floors, white walls, classical pillars, and swiveling cherry wood dividers are the fundamental elements of this 4,000-square foot space. Divided into two equal halves—public and private—by a large swinging panel with a translucent window that transmits light, the whole space is an interesting play of light on plane surfaces, walls, and floors. Some pieces of furniture have geometric indentations that are sometimes aesthetic, at other times functional gestures. The interaction between lines, clarity, and varied materials plays a unique role in this dwelling and its perception of space.

Für einen jungen Banker ist dieser Soho-Loft ein ruhiger Ort, um sich vom Trubel der Stadt zurückzuziehen. Helle Holzböden, weiße Wände, klassische Säulen und drehbare Kirschholz-Raumteiler sind die Hauptelemente auf 370 m^2 Grundfläche. Der gesamte Raum ist mittels einer beweglichen Wandscheibe mit einem Fenster, durch das Tageslicht einfällt, in zwei gleichgroße Hälften aufgeteilt – eine öffentliche und eine private – und bietet ein interessantes Lichtspiel auf den glatten Oberflächen, Wänden und Böden. Einige Möbel haben geometrische, teils ästhetische, teils funktionelle Einkerbungen. Dem Spiel zwischen Umrissen, Helligkeit und Materialien kommt in dieser Wohnung und ihrer Raumwahrnehmung eine besondere Rolle zu.

Foyer d'un jeune banquier, ce loft de Soho est une retraite paisible, loin du tumulte de la ville. Parquets en bois clair, murs blancs, piliers classiques et séparations pivotantes en cerisier sont les éléments fondamentaux de cet espace de 370 m^2. Divisé en deux moitiés - public et privé - par un grand panneau pivotant, doté d'une fenêtre translucide laissant passer la lumière, l'ensemble de l'espace est un captivant jeu de lumière avec les surfaces planes, les murs et le sol. Certains meubles comprennent des indentations géométriques, signes esthétiques parfois, d'autres fois fonctionnels. L'interaction entre lignes, clarté et matériaux variés joue un rôle singulier dans cette demeure, et sa perception de l'espace.

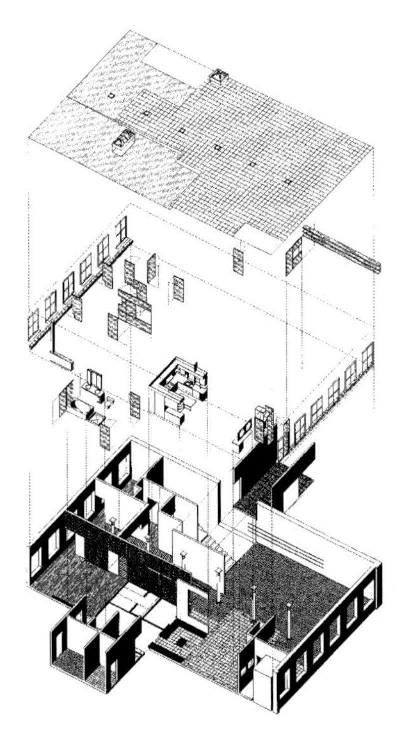

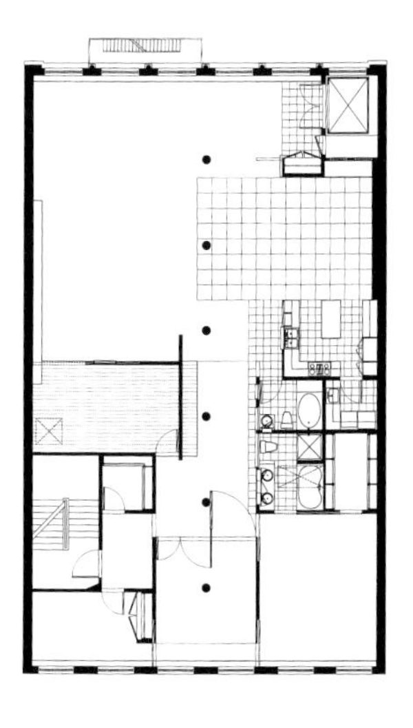

The dining room and kitchen are defined by pillars that run down the middle of the space. Curved shapes contrasts with larger linear structures.

Das Esszimmer und die Küche werden von Säulen markiert, die durch die Raummitte verlaufen. Geschwungene Formen kontrastieren mit größeren linearen Strukturen.

La salle à manger et la cuisine sont définies par des piliers qui parcourent la moitié de l'espace. Des formes curvilignes contrastent avec des structures linéaires, plus grande.

Vicente Wolf Loft

Vicente Wolf

Photos: © Vicente Wolf
Completion date: 1998

The interior design of this loft outshines its architectural details. The space is a constantly evolving setting where the designer and owner can experiment with objects that he enjoys. Travelling two months out of the year, Wolf returns loaded with new objects. He treats his home as an empty canvas, adding and combining pieces that come together effortlessly to create a multi-faceted atmosphere. An impressive collection of 20th century photography hangs on the walls and windowpanes. Imposing sculptural works, precious objects from the New York flea market, an 18th century chair, a Luis XVI bench, a 19th century table, and other relics from the 40's and 50's adorn the sophisticated and free environment.

Hier überstrahlt die Einrichtung die architektonischen Details. Nach Aussage des Gestalters und Eigentümers ist der Loft ein Rahmen konstanter Veränderung, in dem er mit den Dingen, die ihm gefallen, experimentieren kann. Nach zweimonatigen Reisen kehrt er Jahr für Jahr mit neuen Objekten beladen zurück. Sein Zuhause ist wie eine leere Leinwand, auf der er die Stücke, die sich wie von selbst ansammeln, nach Belieben hinzufügen und kombinieren kann, um eine facettenreiche Atmosphäre zu schaffen. Eine eindrucksvolle Foto-Sammlung des 20. Jahrhunderts überzieht Wände und Fenster. Skulpturen und kostbare Einzelstücke verschiedener Epochen von den New Yorker Flohmärkten dekorieren dieses raffinierte und liberale Zuhause.

La conception intérieure de ce loft éclipse ses détails architecturaux. Selon le designer, et propriétaire, l'espace est un décor en perpétuelle évolution, pour expérimenter à l'aide de ses objets de prédilection. En voyage pendant deux mois de l'année, Wolf revient chargé de nouveaux objets. Son appartement est une toile vide, sur laquelle il ajoute et associe des éléments qui s'emboîtent sans effort, créant une atmosphère à multiples facettes. Une collection spectaculaire de photographies XXe orne les murs et les fenêtres. Sculptures imposantes, objets précieux dénichés sur le marché aux puces de New York, une chaise XVIIIe, une banquette Louis XVI, une table XIXe et d'autres antiquités des années 40 et 50 embellissent ce lieu libre, et sophistiqué.

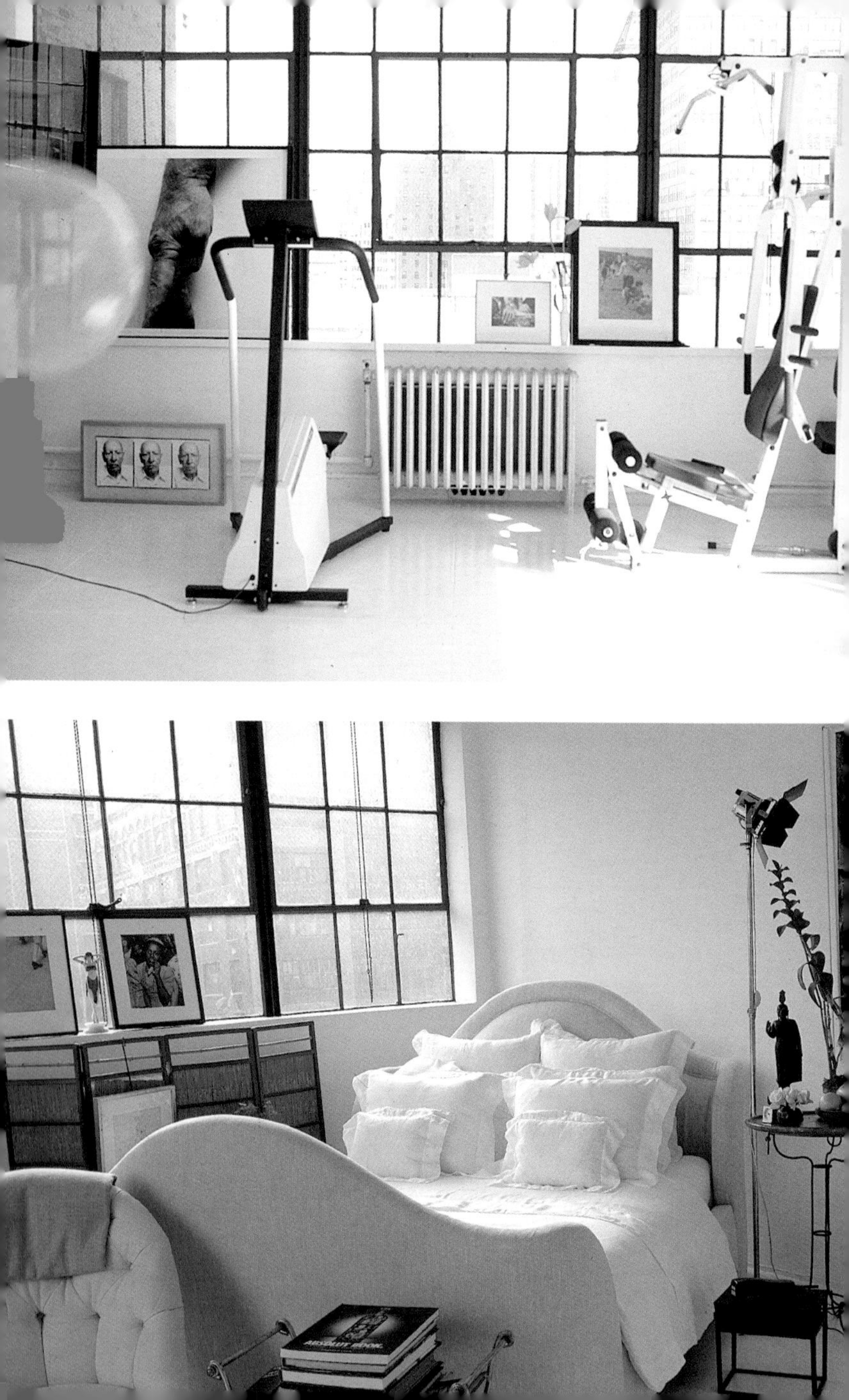

Holley Loft

Hanrahan & Meyers

Photos: © Peter Aaron / Esto
Completion date: 1995

This loft apartment located on the second floor of a Manhattan building is a cohesive open space of overlapping areas linked to one another through a series of panels and planes. While walls define the boundaries of rooms, movable panels and planes made of transparent glass and steel frames discreetly divide the space into the different areas that continuously meld into each other. Pillars divide the space into public and private zones. Exposed pipes were restored and maintained as decorative elements. A solid steel wall masks the freight elevator, while maple wood is the predominant material which gives the smooth texture and warm tonal quality to this highly urban residence.

Dieser Loft, in der zweiten Etage eines Gebäudes in Manhattan gelegen, ist ein zusammenhängender offener Raum sich überlagernder Abschnitte, die durch Paneele und Ebenen miteinander verbunden sind. Weiße Wände ziehen die Zimmergrenzen, bewegliche Tafeln und durchsichtige Glasscheiben in Stahlrahmen untergliedern das Apartment diskret in die verschiedenen Bereiche, die kontinuierlich verschmelzen. Eine massive Stahlwand kaschiert den Lastenaufzug; Ahornholz ist das vorherrschende Material und verleiht diesem stark urbanen Zuhause eine sanfte Oberflächenstruktur und warme Farben.

Ce loft situé au deuxième d'un immeuble de Manhattan est un espace ouvert uni, constitué d'environnements superposés et reliés entre eux par une série de cloisons et de plans. Les murs définissant les limites des pièces, des panneaux et séparateurs mobiles, en verre transparent et encadrés d'acier, divisent discrètement l'espace en différentes aires s'entremêlant. Un mur massif d'acier masque le monte-charge et l'érable, matériau prédominant, confère une texture fluide et une tonalité chaleureuse à cette résidence très urbaine.

Morton Loft

Lot/Ek

Photos: © Paul Warchol
Completion date: 1999
info@lotekarchitecture.com

This original loft incorporates a petroleum trailer tank that encapsulates the private areas, leaving the surrounding space undivided. The tank was elevated and inserted into the fourth floor of a former parking garage and cut into two sections. One section was placed horizontally over the living room to isolate two sleeping pods. Two large hatchback doors connected to hydraulic pistons open electrically to let in sunlight and ventilation. The other section was placed vertically from floor to ceiling and contains two bathrooms, one on top of the other. A system of metal grating catwalks, filled with clear resin, provides access to the upper bathroom, sleeping pods, and closets on either side.

Zum originellen Loft gehört der alte Anhänger eines Tankwagens, der die privaten Bereiche einkapselt und den Rest des Raumes frei lässt. Der Tank wurde in die vierte Etage eines ehemaligen Parkhauses eingebaut und in zwei Teile geteilt. Ein Teil wurde horizontal über dem Wohnzimmer angebracht, um die beiden Schlafkammern zu isolieren. Zwei breite Hecktüren mit hydraulischen Kolben öffnen sich elektrisch, um Sonnenlicht und Frischluft hereinzulassen. Der andere Teil des Tanks wurde vertikal zwischen Boden und Decke aufgestellt und enthält zwei Badezimmer, eins über dem anderen. Metallene Gitter-Laufstege, die mit klarem Harz ausgegossen sind, erschließen das obere Bad, die Schlafkammern und Schränke an den Seiten.

Ce loft original incorpore une citerne à essence, ceignant les aires privées et laissant l'espace alentour sans division. Le réservoir a été introduit au quatrième étage d'un ancien garage, et coupé en deux sections. L'une, placée à l'horizontale au-dessus du séjour, isole les cabines de couchage. Deux grands hayons connectés à des pistons hydrauliques s'ouvrent électriquement pour laisser passer lumière du jour et ventilation. L'autre section est à la verticale, du sol au plafond, et abrite deux salles de bain, l'une au-dessus de l'autre. Un système de passerelles grillagées de métal, emplies de résine claire, offre un accès aux couchages et placards et à la salle de bain supérieure, de chaque côté.

The introduction of a petroleum tanker defines the raw characteristics of this loft. These innovative structures not only isolate the rooms, but also stand alone as impressive structures that shape the home's personality. The loft´s industrial quality is played up by glossy blue floors and cherry red furniture.

Der Einbau eines alten Öltanks prägt den rauen Charakter dieses Lofts. Diese innovativen Elemente trennen nicht nur Räume voneinander, sondern sind auch beeindruckende Skulpturen. Der industrielle Look des Lofts wird durch den glänzenden blauen Boden und kirschrote Möbel belebt.

L'introduction d'une citerne à essence signifie la nature brute de ce loft. Ces structures novatrices non seulement isolent les pièces, mais constituent également des éléments singuliers formant la personnalité du lieu. Le caractère industriel du loft est souligné par des sols bleu brillant et un mobilier rouge cerise.

Loft on the Hudson River

Peter Tow

Photos: © Björg
Completion date: 1999

Surrounded by an industrial area that leads to the Holland Tunnel connecting Manhattan to New Jersey, this loft was once a commercial space for heavy machinery. To balance its former use with the current one, the architects created a clean and luminous interior, laying down maple wood floors and French limestone. Sandblasted glass partitions separate the bedrooms from the living areas, permitting light to flow throughout the loft. Whitewashed walls and concrete beams accompany maple wood furniture, and the setting is a neutral canvas for special objects and beautiful rugs. The kitchen uses wood and stainless steel, and its ample windows provide fantastic views of the old industrial neighborhood of Tribeca.

Dieser Loft, umgeben von einem Industriegebiet, war einst Handelsplatz für schwere Maschinen. Um zwischen der ursprünglichen und der neuen Nutzung einen Ausgleich herzustellen, schufen die Architekten helle, reine Innenräume, indem sie Ahornholz und französischen Kalkstein auf dem Boden verlegten. Sandgestrahlte Glaswände trennen die Schlafzimmer von den Wohnbereichen, Tageslicht kann jedoch den gesamten Loft erhellen. Getünchte Wände und Betonträger harmonieren mit Ahornholzmöbeln; die Anordnung ist ein neutraler Hintergrund für schöne Objekte und Teppiche. In der Küche wurden Holz und Edelstahl verarbeitet, und das breite Fenster bietet phantastische Ausblicke auf das industriell geprägte Stadtviertel Tribeca.

Au sein d'une zone industrielle qui mène au tunnel de Holland, reliant Manhattan au New Jersey, ce loft surplombant l'Hudson était autrefois un espace commercial pour l'industrie. Pour équilibrer ses fonctions passée et présente, les architectes ont créé un intérieur net et lumineux, sur un parterre en érable et en comblanchien. Des cloisons en verre sablé séparent les chambres des aires de vie, tout en laissant la lumière circuler dans tout le loft. Murs blanchis et piliers de béton accompagnent un mobilier en érable. Le décor est une toile neutre offerte aux objets spéciaux et aux tapis somptueux. Les grandes fenêtres d'une cuisine en acier inox et bois proposent de fan-tastiques points de vue sur l'ancien quartier industriel de Tribeca.

0
5
10

The original trabeated system of beams was left intact and painted over in white. Translucent screens diffuse natural light into the bedroom. A unique kitchen counter stands out from the stainless steel kitchen.

Die ursprünglichen Deckenbalken wurden freigelegt und weiß gestrichen. Semi-transparente Wandschirme verteilen das Tageslicht im Schlafzimmer, und eine einzigartige Theke hebt sich von der Edelstahl-Küche ab.

Le système original de poutres en entablement a été laissé intact et repeint en blanc. Des écrans translucides diffusent la lumière naturelle dans la chambre. Un comptoir de cuisine exceptionnel se distingue de la cuisine en acier inox.

Bargmann Loft

Jay Bargmann and Stephanie Goto/RVA

Photos: © Jeff Goldberg / Esto
Completion date: 2000
jgreenberg@rvapc.com

The activities carried out in this apartment define the program of this space and point to the selective materials used which form a cohesive design that is pure and minimalist. The rippling texture of the ebonized oak floors mimics the flowing Hudson River just beyond the window. Chalky white walls, crisp columns and beams reflect the changing light throughout the day. Concrete was used for a cast in place trough sink and kitchen counter. Storage units are revealed only when used. Sculpture-like speakers define the listening area, the bath is behind vertically cantilevered acid etched glass, a 12-foot solid oak table lies in the dining area, and a low oak platform sustains the bed. Black, white and steel predominate.

Die durchgeführten Eingriffe legen das Raumprogramm fest und weisen auf die ausgesuchten Materialien hin, die ein zusammenhängendes reines und minimalistisches Design bilden. Die geriffelte Oberfläche der geschwärzten Eichenböden ahmt den unter dem Fenster vorbeifließenden Hudson River nach. Kalkweiße Wände, Säulen und Balken reflektieren das sich im Tagesverlauf verändernde Licht. Vor Ort wurden die Spüle sowie die Küchentheke aus Beton gegossen. Stauraum wird nur sichtbar, wenn er benutzt wird. Das Bad versteckt sich hinter geätztem Glas, ein 3,50 Meter langer solider Eichentisch steht im Esszimmer und auf einem niedrigen Eichenpodest ruht das Bett. Schwarz, weiß und Stahl dominieren.

Les activités entreprises dans cet appartement définissent la composition de l'espace et soulignent les matériaux sélectifs, formant la cohérence d'un design pur et minimaliste. La texture ondulée des parquets en chêne noirci imite le courant de l'Hudson, au-delà de la fenêtre. Murs blanc craie, colonnes et poutres nettes reflètent la lumière changeant avec le cours de la journée. Évier et comptoir de cuisine en béton ont été coulés sur place. Les rangements apparaissent uniquement lorsqu'ils sont utilisés. Des sculptures/haut-parleurs définissent la zone d'audition, le bain est derrière des vitres dépolies à l'acide suspendues, une table de 3,50 m habite la salle à manger et le lit repose sur un dais en chêne. Noir, blanc et acier prédominent.

Kaplen Loft

Robert Marino

Photos: © Dan Bibb
Completion date: 1998

Instead of a typical New York City apartment divided into small rooms, this living space offers a roughly square area with open views to the east and west, as well as high ten-foot ceilings inside a 3,500 square foot space. The home's most distinguishing element is found on the ceiling, where heating and cooling systems hide beneath large rings made of stretched rolled aluminum. Their shape and presence establishes the structures and shapes of the fluid space. Walls are fitted into these circular sockets, forming uniquely concaved free-standing structures. Doors are fabricated from skin panels. Bold primary colors accompany the gray stone floors and cyprus wood cabinetry.

Statt der üblichen Aufgliederung in kleine Räume bietet diese New Yorker Wohnung auf 325 m^2 eine nahezu quadratische Fläche mit freiem Blick nach Osten und Westen sowie drei Meter hohen Decken. Das auffälligste Element dieses Apartments befindet sich an der Decke, wo sich die Installationen der Heizung und der Klimaanlage unter großen Kreisen aus gespanntem und gerolltem Aluminium verstecken. Ihre Form und Präsenz bildet die Struktur und Gestalt des fließenden Raumes. Die Wände und Säulen wurden diesen kreisförmigen Öffnungen angepasst und bilden einzigartige freistehende Elemente. Kräftige Primärfarben begleiten den grauen Steinfußboden und die Schränke aus Zypressenholz.

Au lieu d'un appartement new-yorkais typique, divisé en petites pièces, ce lieu de vie propose un espace presque carré de 325 m^2 doté de larges vues sur l'est et l'ouest, et de plafonds à plus de trois mètres. L'élément le plus caractéristique se trouve précisément au plafond, où la tuyauterie se cache sous de grands cercles de laminé aluminium. Leur silhouette et leur aspect asseyent structures et formes de l'espace fluide. Les murs s'inscrivent dans ces ouvertures circulaires, formant des structures libres exceptionnelles. D'audacie-uses couleurs primaires accompagnent les sols de pierre et le mobilier en bois de Chypre.

Malin Residence

Resolution: 4

Photos: © Peter Margonelli, © Peter Mauss/Esto, © Paul Warchol
Completion date: 1999
jtanney@re4a.com

Over the years, many of the classic pre-war apartments of New York have been butchered; their ample interiors compartmentalized into numerous rooms and narrow hallways. In order to restore this apartment's original splendor and to create a sense of order, the architects inserted a central void in the form of an oval, which carves out a space that contains the dining room and leads to the other areas of the house. The client calls it a `rotary circle´ that serves as a circulation system, creating specific and sequential relationships between public zones. The neutral colors and selected materials, including maple wood, black slate and granite, glass, and aluminum, produce a comfortable and clean-cut environment.

Im Laufe der Jahre sind viele Vorkriegswohnungen zerstückelt worden: die weitläufigen Räume wurden in zahlreiche Zimmer und enge Flure aufgeteilt. Um den ursprünglichen Glanz dieses Apartments wieder herzustellen und eine neue Ordnung einzuführen, bauten die Architekten einen zentralen ovalen Freiraum ein, der einen Teil des Esszimmers einnimmt und die anderen Bereiche des Hauses miteinander verknüpft. Der Bauherr nennt ihn "Rotationskreis"; er dient als Zirkulationssystem und stellt besondere Beziehungen zwischen den einzelnen Zonen her. Neutrale Farben sowie ausgewählte Baustoffe - Ahornholz, Schiefer, Granit, Glas und Aluminium - schaffen eine komfortable und klar umrissene Einrichtung.

Au fil des années, nombre d'appartements typiques de l'avant guerre ont été saccagés, leurs vastes intérieurs compartimentés en de nombreuses pièces et couloirs étroits. Pour restaurer la splendeur originelle du lieu, et créer une sensation d'ordre, les architectes ont introduit un vide central de forme ovale, qui sculpte un espace accueillant la salle à manger et menant aux autres parties de la demeure. Le client l'appelle «sens giratoire», servant de système de circulation et créant des relations précises et séquentielles entre les zones communes. Les couleurs neutres et les matériaux choisis tels l'érable, l'ardoise noire, le granit, le verre et l'aluminium, engendrent un environnement confortable et soigné.

GREAT GOOD FOOD

Frank and Amy's Loft

Resolution: 4

Photos: © Paul Warchol
Completion date: 2000
jtanney@re4a.com

This wide-open space in a former industrial building was designed for an art critic and film editor. The loft's stylishly unkempt interior fits in with the nature of the gritty neighborhood, Hell's Kitchen. A dense, complex box contains the kitchen, mechanical and secondary spaces and separates them from the public and private areas. Huge sliding doors allow the bedrooms to be closed off. The architect enhanced industrial features such as the ceiling tubes and the sanded concrete floors. Curious and colorful objects complement the overlapping rugs underneath numerous ceiling spotlights. A mixture of contemporary and retro elements tones down the loft's industrial quality and lightens and brightens the atmosphere.

Dieser weite offene Raum in einem alten Industriegebäude wurde für einen Kunstkritiker und Filmemacher geplant. Die stilisierte und nachlässige Einrichtung passt gut zum Charakter des ruppigen Viertels, Hell's Kitchen. Eine Box birgt die Küche sowie Technik- und Nebenräume und isoliert sie von Gesellschaftszonen und privaten Bereichen. Das Schlafzimmer kann durch Schiebetüren verschlossen werden. Der Architekt hob ein paar industrielle Merkmale hervor, wie Rohrleitungen und geschmirgelte Betonböden. Kuriosa und bunte Objekte runden die von zahlreichen Spots beleuchteten Teppiche ab. Die Mischung aus modernen und Retro-Elementen mildert den industriellen Look des Lofts und lockert die Stimmung.

Cet espace grand ouvert dans un ancien bâtiment industriel a été conçu pour un critique d'art et un monteur. L'intérieur au négligé stylisé du loft convient parfaitement au quartier dur de Hell's Kitchen. Un module dense et complexe comprend la cuisine, les équipements et les espaces secondaires, et les sépare des aires privées et publiques. D'immenses portes coulissantes permettent de fermer les chambres. L'architecte a mis en relief les éléments industriels, tels la tuyauterie au plafond et les sols en béton poncé. Sous les spots, des objets étranges et hauts en couleur s'ajoutent aux tapis qui se chevauchent. L'aspect industriel du lieu est adouci par un mélange d'éléments contemporains et rétros, qui illumine et avive l'atmosphère.

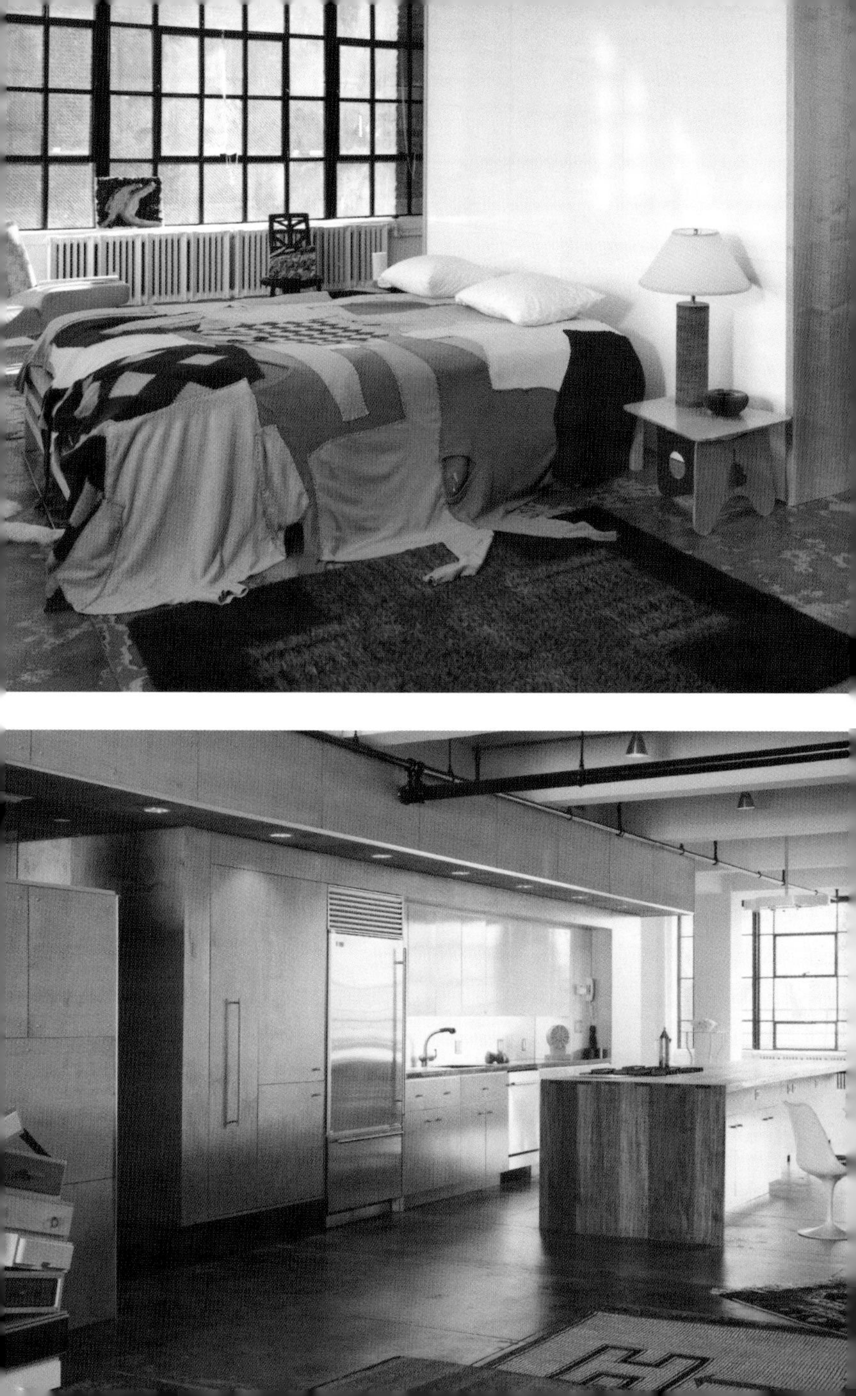

Potter's Loft

Resolution: 4

Photos: © Eduard Hueber
Completion date: 1999
jtanney@re4a.com

Located in New York's Chelsea district, this rectangular loft is characterized by its use of various materials to identify the different areas. The front door is a sliding metal panel that conceals access from the elevator and stairway. Comfortable couches sit in the living area at the right, and on the left are the dining room and kitchen with a square black panel fireplace. Overhead, strips of light crowd the ceiling at perpendicular angles, and a unique wedge light protrudes from the center. Behind a practical pivoting door are the bedroom and bathroom. Wood floors, cleaned brick walls, metal surfaces, and unusual lighting characterize this linear space that offers both visible and tangible elements.

Im Stadtteil Chelsea zeichnet sich dieser rechteckige Loft durch den Einsatz zahlreicher Materialien aus, um verschiedene Bereiche einzufassen. Die Eingangstür ist eine verschiebbare Metallplatte, die den Zugang vom Fahrstuhl und Treppenhaus abschirmt. Bequeme Sofas stehen im auf der rechten Seite gelegenen Wohnzimmer, linker Hand liegen Esszimmer und Küche mit einem quadratischen schwarzen Herd. Über den Köpfen winden sich Lichtstrahlen in rechten Winkeln entlang, und eine einzigartige Keil-Lampe ragt aus der Mitte. Hinter einer praktischen Schiebetür liegen Schlafzimmer und Bad. Holzböden, blankes Mauerwerk, Metalloberflächen und ungewöhnliche Beleuchtung charakterisieren diesen geradliniegen Raum.

Situé à New York dans le quartier de Chelsea, ce loft rectangulaire se caractérise par l'utilisation de divers matériels pour identifier les différentes espaces. Un panneau de métal coulissant sert de porte d'entrée, dissimulant un accès à l'ascenseur et à l'escalier. À droite des divans confortables dans le séjour, et à gauche la salle à manger et la cuisine, dotée d'une hotte sur un plan de travail noir. En l'air des rubans de lumière perpendiculaires peuplent le plafond, une seule lampe en forme de coin émergeant au centre. Audelà d'une porte pivotante pratique se trouvent la chambre et la salle de bain. Parquets, murs de briques nets, surfaces de métal et éclairage insolite caractérisent cet espace linéaire offrant des éléments à la fois visibles et tangibles.

The unique lighting system made up of random rectangular planes remains loyal to the many linear features found throughout the apartment. The walls and floors offer different textures and materials, from smooth white walls and polished wooden floors to industrial metal panels and rough brick surfaces.

Die einzigartige Beleuchtung aus willkürlich zusammengestellten Rechtecken entspricht den vielen geradlinigen Elementen im Apartment. Wände und Böden bieten verschiedene Texturen und Materialien,von soften weißen Wänden und polierten Holzböden bis zu industriell aussehenden Metallplatten und rauen Ziegeloberflächen.

Le système d'éclairage, unique en son genre, fait de plans rectangulaires aléatoires reste fidèle aux caractéristiques linéaires de l'ensemble de l'appartement. Murs et sols offrent différentes textures et matériaux, de parois blanches et lisses et de parquets cirés à des panneaux de métal industriels et des surfaces de brique brute.

Hill Loft

Resolution: 4

Photos: © Eduard Hueber
Completion date: 1999
jtanney@re4a.com

This loft lacked abundant space and was remodeled to take full advantage of every square inch. The gestures were simple: gigantic wall units accommodate the kitchen, a storage area, the dining room, display cabinets, and sleeping and living areas. Each area is separated from the other by way of massive steel plate columns across the eastern wall. Wood and steel are set against white walls that retain their industrial origins. Simple furniture and wood floors provide a neutral background and an uncluttered environment, while the textured white walls and ceiling show off the apartment's most remarkable feature: curved light rails overhead that unwind and intersect gracefully from north to south.

Da der Raum in diesem Loft knapp war, wurde er durch ein paar einfache Kunstgriffe umgestaltet, um jeden Quadratzentimeter auszunutzen: riesige Wandteile gliedern Küche, Stauraum, Essplatz, Vitrinen, Schlaf- und Wohnbereiche. Die einzelnen Abschnitte sind durch massive stahlüberzogene Säulen entlang der östlichen Wand voneinander getrennt. Holz und Stahl heben sich von weißen Wänden ab, die an ihre industrielle Herkunft erinnern. Schlichte Möbel und Holzböden bilden einen neutralen Hintergrund, während die strukturierten Wände und Decken die auffälligsten Details des Apartments präsentieren: geschwungene Lampenseile, die sich von Nord nach Süd und überschneidend an der Decke entlangwinden.

En déficit d'espace, ce loft a été remodelé pour tirer pleinement parti de chaque centimètre carré. Les mesures ont été simples: des pans de mur gigantesques accueillent la cuisine, un espace rangement, la salle à manger, des vitrines et les aires de vie et de repos. Chaque zone est séparée de l'autre par des colonnes en plaques d'acier en travers du mur est. Le bois et l'acier contrebalancent les murs blancs qui préservent les origines industrielles. Mobilier simple et parquets offrent un fond neutre, les murs blancs texturés et le plafond mettant en lumière la caractéristique la plus remarquable du lieu: un éclairage au plafond monté sur des rails curvilignes, qui se croisent et s'entrecroisent, du nord au sud.

Moody Residence

Resolution: 4

Photos: © Paul Warchol
Completion date: 1998
jtanney@re4a.com

Two two-bedroom apartments were joined to create one four-bedroom, full floor apartment with direct access to an elevator and 360 degree views of the city. The apartment is divided into public and private zones, and the south side contains the kitchen, dining room, and living area. The kitchen island, with an incorporated dining table, both unifies and separates the cooking and entertainment areas. The north side houses the bedrooms, where the master bedroom suite, fitted with wooden closets and built-in dressers, has its own bathroom with a large open shower. Wood interiors, white and black surfaces, and a few warm colors characterize the interiors, natural light permeates the entire space.

Zwei Zwei-Zimmer-Apartments wurden zu einer Vier-Zimmer-Wohnung über die gesamte Etage mit direktem Zugang zu einem Fahrstuhl und 360°-Ausblicken auf die Stadt zusammengeschlossen. Gesellschafts- und private Bereiche sind getrennt; im südlichen Abschnitt liegen Küche, Esszimmer und Wohnraum. Die Kücheninsel mit eingebautem Esstisch vereint und trennt Koch- und Freizeitbereich. Im Norden befindet sich das Schlafzimmer mit Holzschränken und begehbaren Kleiderschränken sowie einem eigenen Badezimmer mit großer, offener Dusche. Holz, schwarze und weiße Oberflächen sowie ein paar warme Farben zeichnen die Einrichtung aus; natürliches Licht erfüllt den gesamten Raum.

Deux appartements de deux chambres ont été réunis pour créer un appartement à quatre chambres, de plain-pied, avec accès direct à l'ascenseur et vue à 360 degrés sur la ville. Le lieu est divisé entre les zones privées et publiques, la partie sud contenant la cuisine, la salle à manger et le séjour. L'îlot cuisine, avec table de repas incorporée, unit et sépare les zones de cuisine et de réception. Le côté nord abrite une chambre, de même que la chambre principale, dotée de placards en bois et d'une commode encastrée, et ses dépendances dont une salle de bain avec une grande douche ouverte. Le design intérieur se caractérise par l'emploi du bois, les surfaces blanches et noires, la lumière naturelle s'insinuant dans l'ensemble de l'espace.

Monolithic Structure

Resolution: 4

Photos: © Paul Warchol
Completion date: 1998
jtanney@re4a.com

The aim of the architects behind this third floor apartment in New York's financial district was to create a continuous, undivided home along a straight line. Long and narrow lofts are typical of New York buildings that were once used for industrial purposes. At one end of the apartment, bedrooms and bathrooms lead through to the kitchen and dining room, and then to the living area, and finally to the studio and guestroom. Partitions are made of Durock panels, and the walls are painted white. Distinguishing features include the foldout projecting bed designed by the architect, overhead railed spotlights, and relief layers across the ceiling that create a unique, textured effect.

Die Architekten wollten in diesem Apartment im dritten Stock des New Yorker Finanzdistriktes eine zusammenhängende, nach einer geraden Linie ausgerichtete Wohnung einrichten. Lange und schmale Lofts sind typisch für die alten New Yorker Industriegebäude. An der einen Seite gelangt man durch Schlafzimmer und Bäder in die Küche und das Esszimmer, dann in den Wohnraum und schließlich in das Arbeits- und Gästezimmer. Raumteiler sind aus 'Durock'-Paneelen; die Wände sind weiß gestrichen. Zu den Besonderheiten gehören das ausklappbare, vom Architekten entworfene Bett, Deckenschienen mit Spots und Reliefschichten an der Decke, die einen einmaligen Struktureffekt hervorrufen.

Pour cet appartement situé au 3e, dans le quartier financier de New York, le but des architectes était de créer un foyer continu et unifié, le long d'une droite stricte. Les lofts longs et étroits sont typiques des immeubles new-yorkais, au passé industriel. À une extrémité du logement, chambres et salles de bain mènent à la cuisine et à la salle à manger, puis à l'aire de séjour, et finalement à l'atelier et à la chambre d'hôte. Les séparations sont en panneaux Durock, les murs peints en blanc. Un lit en strates projetées conçu par l'architecte, des spots sur rail et des couches en relief au plafond, créant un effet de texture unique, sont les traits distinctifs de cet appartement.

Spotlights are fixed onto a maze of pipes that float underneath the geometrical patterns created by the relief layers of the ceiling. The spotlights are pointed towards the ceiling to grant a comfortable, indirect light over the living area. The kitchen table incorporates useful storage space.

Strahler sind auf einem Geflecht von Rohren angebracht, das unter dem geometrischen Muster der Deckenreliefs schwebt. Die Lampen sind auf die Decke gerichtet, um den Wohnbereich komfortabel indirekt zu beleuchten, und im Küchentisch steckt nützlicher Stauraum.

Des spots sont fixés sur un labyrinthe de tuyaux, flottant sous des motifs géométriques créés par les reliefs du plafond. Les projecteurs pointent vers le plafond, proposant une lumière indirecte confortable sur toute la zone. La table de cuisine est dotée de rangements pratiques.

Executives' Apartment

Frank Lupo and Daniel Rowen

Photos: © Michael Moran
Completion date: 1998

In an attempt to avoid the daily frantic commute, two Wall Street stockbrokers decided to build a home from where they could also work. The result is a double-level space in which the rooms are connected but do not interfere with each other acoustically. Sophisticated computer and communications systems are located in the office area. Monitors are scattered throughout the home so that the stockbrokers can watch them from the kitchen and corridor. Floor-to-ceiling windows and paneling along the corridor walls add light and dimension. A steel staircase and the tones provided by maple wood, marble, granite, and translucent glass all contribute to the project's original character.

Als Versuch, der täglichen frenetischen Hektik zu entgehen, richteten zwei Wall Street Broker eine Wohnung ein, in der sie auch arbeiten können. Das Ergebnis ist ein Apartment mit doppelter Raumhöhe, in dem die verschiedenen Bereiche miteinander verbunden sind, sich jedoch akustisch nicht stören. Das Büro ist mit modernsten Computer- und Kommunikationssystemen ausgestattet. Monitore bevölkern die Wohnung, so dass die Aktienhändler sie von Küche und Flur einsehen können. Fenstertüren mit Blick auf die Stadt lassen Tageslicht herein und Paneele geben Struktur. Die Stahltreppe zur oberen Ebene, die Farbtöne des Ahornholzes, des Marmors, des Granits und Glas tragen zum originellen Charakter des Entwurfs bei.

Essayant d'éviter les infernaux trajets de banlieue quotidiens, deux agents de change ont décidé de construire un foyer où ils pourraient aussi travailler. Le résultat: un espace à deux niveaux dont les chambres communiquent sans pour autant interférer entre elles acoustiquement. Moyens de communication et ordinateur sophistiqué sont situés dans la zone bureau. Des écrans sont dispersés dans toute la maison, afin que les résidents puissent les consulter dans la cuisine ou le couloir. Les hautes fenêtres donnant sur la ville baignent l'appartement de lumière naturelle, les lambris sur les murs du couloir ajoutant de la dimension. L'escalier en acier menant à l'étage, et les tons issus du bois d'érable, du marbre, du granit et du verre translucide, contribuent à la personnalité originale du projet.

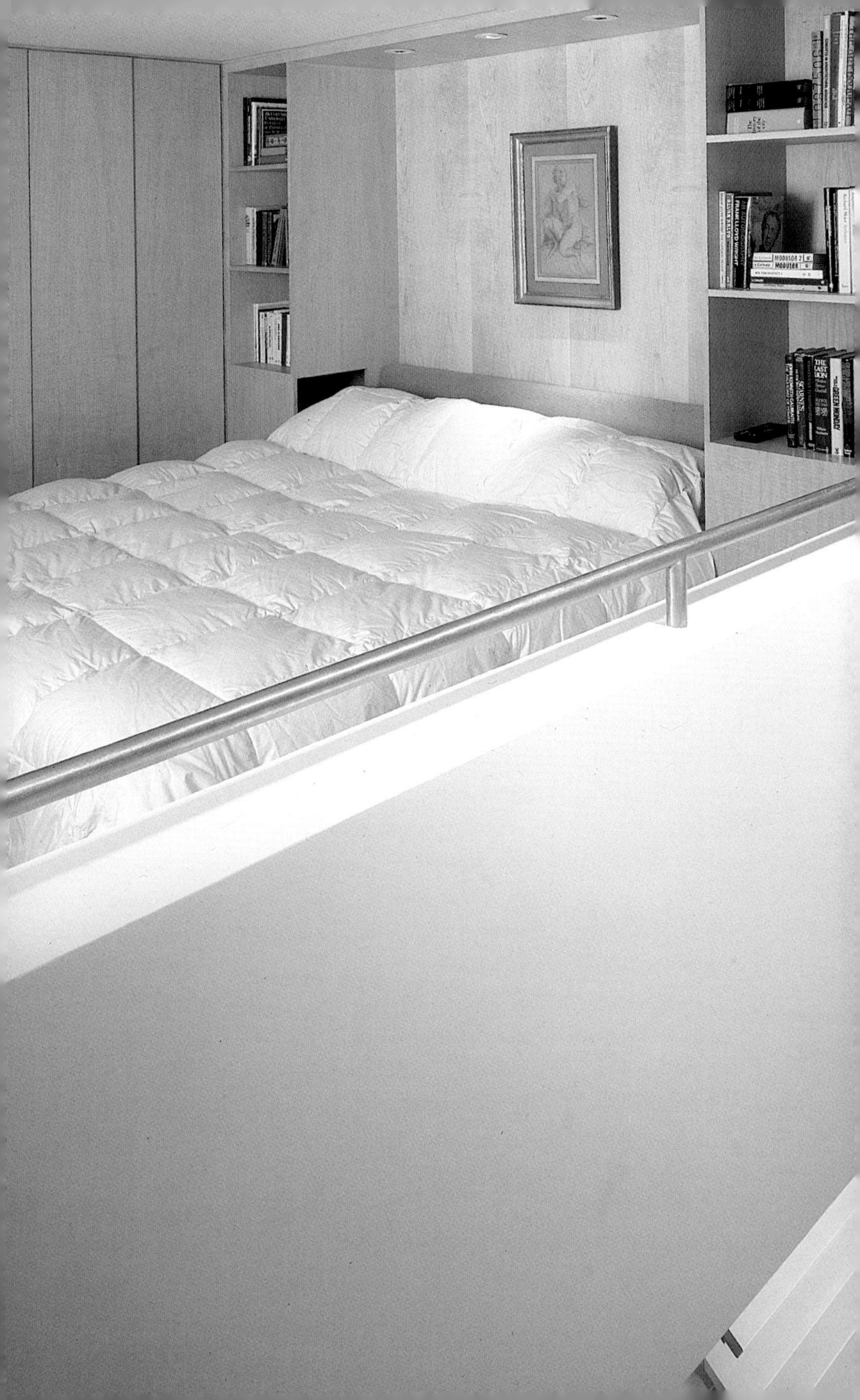
FRANK LLOYD WRIGHT
MODULOR 2
MODULOR
THE LAST LION
GREEN MONDAY

Private Apartment

Frank Lupo and Daniel Rowen

Photos: © Michael Moran
Completion date: 1997

This floating white haven uses techniques that set it apart from most of its minimalist counterparts. The space is not `unfurnished´. On the contrary, the client, attracted to the play of light against the multiple planes of the walls, floors, and ceilings, is responsible for its bareness. A pure white pal-ette, translucent screens and doors and partition walls slightly elevated from the floor give the space a sensation of lightness and mobility. Translucent fabric screens are used instead of windows to filter the space and to isolate it visually from the exterior. This celestial dwelling, a dramatic contrast to the restlessness and bustle of Manhattan, invites meditation and radiates energy, light, and calm.

Die in diesem weißen 'Himmel' eingesetzten Techniken grenzen sich von den meis-ten minimalistischen Einrichtungen ab. Der Raum ist nicht 'unmöbliert'. Der Bauherr, verführt vom Spiel des Lichts auf den vielfältigen Ebenen der Wände, Böden und Decken, ist selbst für die Nacktheit verantwortlich. Reines weiß, durchscheinende Wandschirme und Türen sowie leicht vom Boden abgehobene Trennwände verleihen dem Raum den Eindruck von Leichtigkeit und Bewegung. Statt Fenster wurden durchscheinende Stoffschirme als Filter und zur Abschirmung nach außen eingesetzt. Diese Wohnung stellt einen starken Kontrast zur Rastlosigkeit Manhattans dar, sie lädt zur Meditation ein und strahlt Energie, Licht und Ruhe aus.

Ce havre de blancheur recourt à des techniques le situant à part de ses homologues minimalistes. L'espace n'est pas `dégarni´, bien au contraire. Le client, souhaitant faire jouer la lumière contre les surfaces planes – murs, sols et plafonds – a opté pour ce dépouillement. Tonalité blanche, cloisons et portes translucides, murs de séparation légèrement surélevés donnent à l'espace une sensation de légèreté et de mouvement. Des écrans translucides remplacent les fenêtres, pour filtrer l'espace et l'isoler visuellement de l'extérieur. Contrepoint spectaculaire à l'agitation et au tumulte de Manhattan, cette demeure céleste, irradiant d'énergie, de lumière et de calme, invite à la méditation.

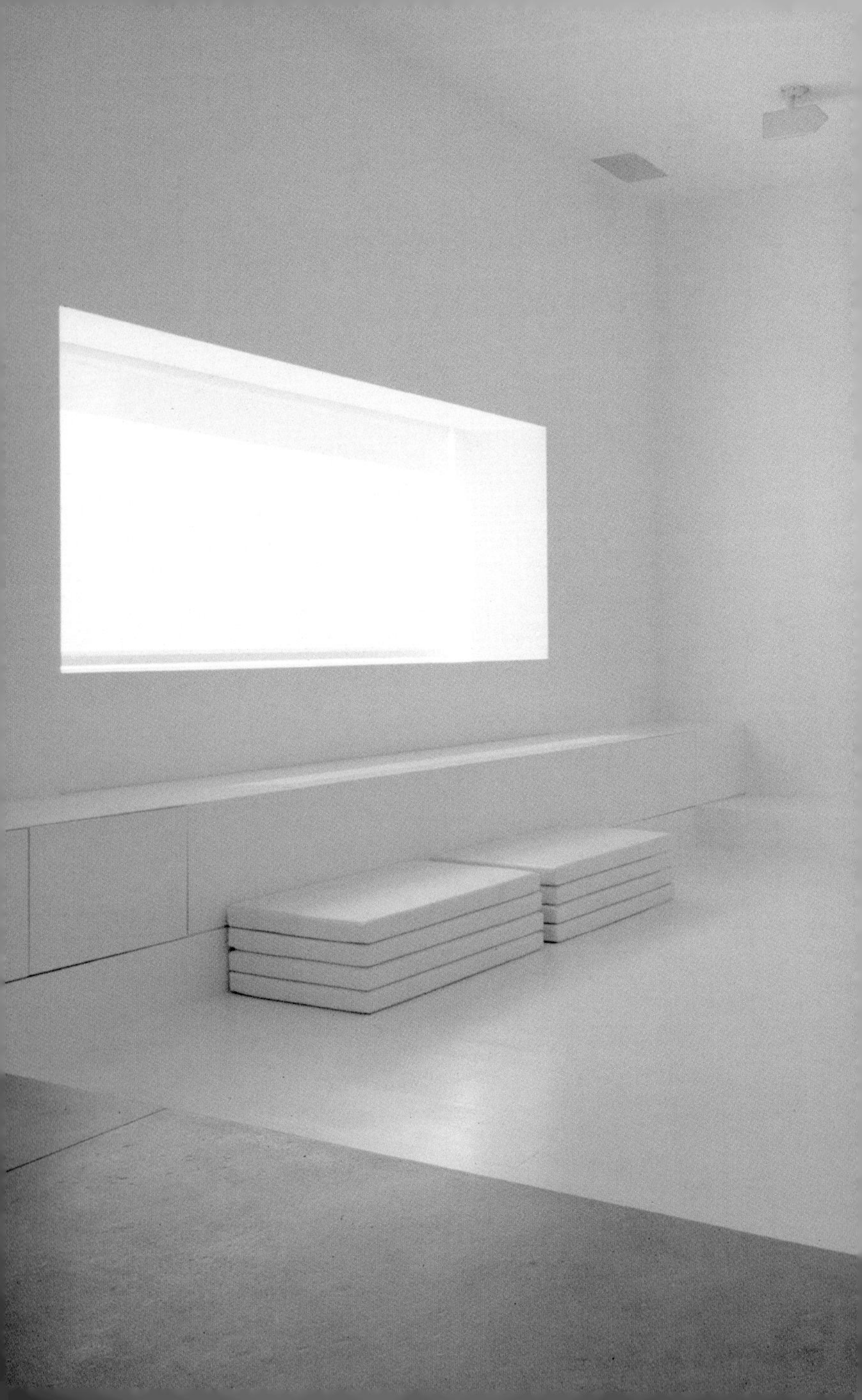

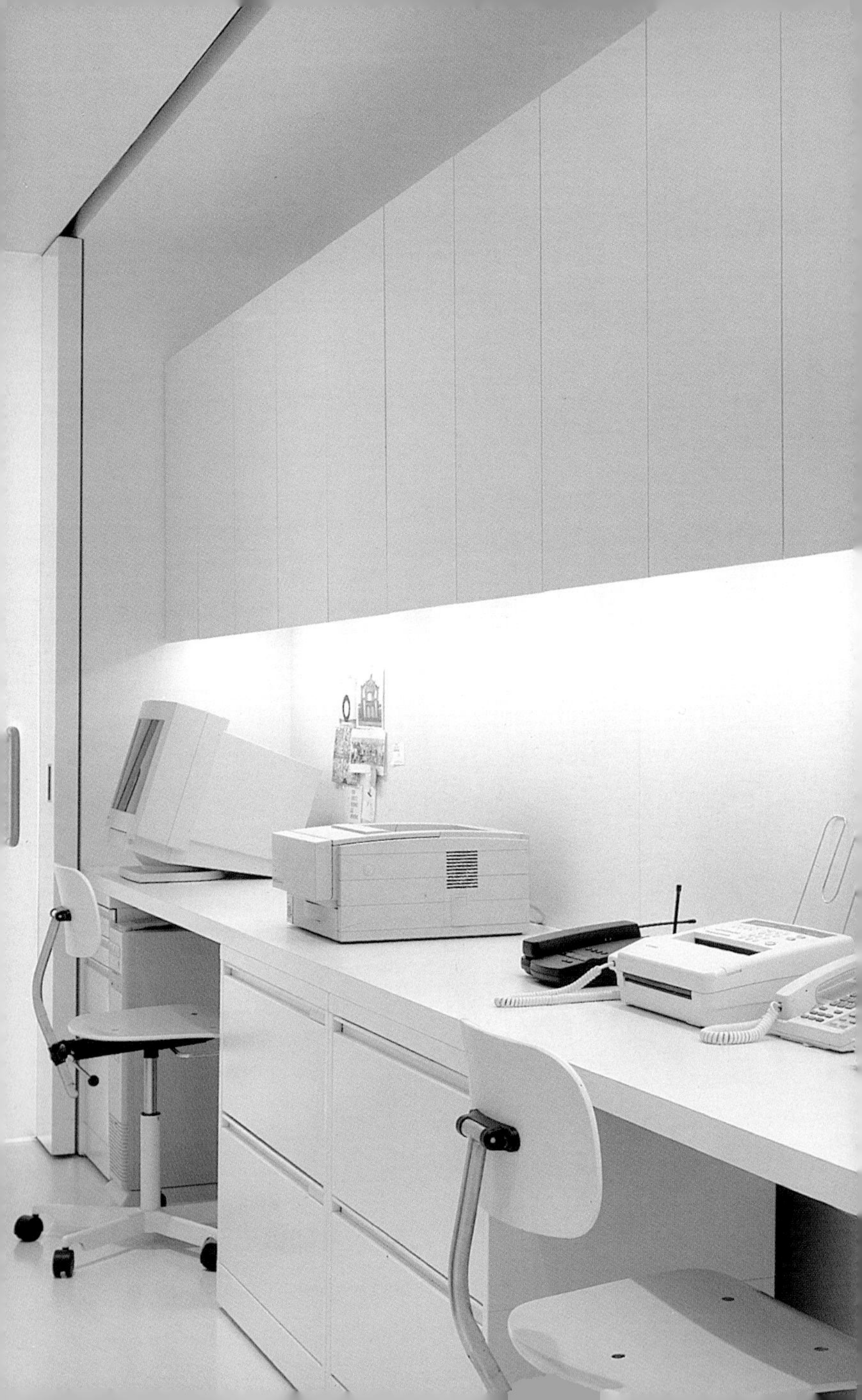

The Siegel-Swansea Loft

Abelow Conners Sherman Architects

Photos: © Michael Moran
Completion date: 1997
dsherman@acsach.net

Originally an early 20th century factory, this space was designed to cater to the needs of a writer-painter couple in New York. Architects preserved the vaulted ceiling, plastered walls, and industrial details, restoring the rest of the space by using similar materials and techniques. In the living room/office, the couple keeps the necessary gear to both work and relax. The bedrooms, bathrooms and a dressing room surround this central unit, while the kitchen, dining room, and living room mingle with the studio, entrance hall, and corridor. The uncrowded space is finished in a neutral gray, on which artwork stands out and can be fully appreciated by the satisfied residents.

Ursprünglich eine Fabrik des frühen 20. Jahrhunderts, wurde dieser Raum nach den Bedürfnissen eines Schriftsteller/Maler-Paares entworfen. Die Architekten bewahrten gewölbte Decken, verputzte Wände und industrielle Details und restaurierten den Rest mit ähnlichen Materialien und Techniken. Große Fenster bieten Panoramablicke vom Wohnraum/Büro, wo das Paar die zum Arbeiten und Entspannen nötigen Dinge aufbewahrt. Schlafzimmer, Bäder und Ankleidezimmer umgeben diese zentral gelegene Einheit; Küche, Ess- und Wohnzimmer teilen sich einen Bereich mit Arbeitszimmer, Eingangsbereich und Flur. Vor dem neutralen Grau hebt sich die Kunst gut ab und kann angemessen wahrgenommen werden .

À l'origine une fabrique début XXe, cet espace a été conçu pour répondre aux nécessités d'un couple écrivain/peintre à New York. Les architectes ont conservé le plafond voûté, les murs de plâtre et les détails industriels, restaurant le reste de l'espace avec de matériaux et des techniques similaires. De grandes fenêtres offre des vues panoramiques depuis le séjour/bureau, où le couple conserve ses équipements de travail et de loisir. Chambres, salles de bain et dressing gravitent autour de cette unité centrale, la cuisine, la salle à manger et le séjour se confondant avec l'atelier, l'entrée et le vestibule. La finition gris neutre de cet espace dégagé met les oeuvres d'art en valeur, permettant aux résidents, comblés, de les apprécier pleinement

BASEBALL
MONARCHS
MEMPHIS
RED SOX
TUE. APR. 15
KATY PARK
WACO, TEX.

Jersey City Loft

Abelow Connors Sherman Architects

Photos: © Michael Moran
Completion date: 1993
dsherman@acsach.net

The originality of this loft designed for a musician and producer comes from the use of diverse materials and construction elements. Formerly a 19th century warehouse/stable, many of its original features were preserved and period pieces were added. The three floors permit vertical and horizontal connections and moveable panels and openings allow certain rooms to be combined. The kitchen, dining room, library, and office are on the first floor, while the bedrooms and recording studio are distributed on the two upper levels. Some of the loft's most distinguishing characteristics include a sloping ceiling, a curved wall, galvanized metal, wooden pillars, and a visible web of overhead beams.

Die Originalität dieses Lofts für einen Musiker und Produzenten ist bedingt durch den Einsatz verschiedenartiger Materialien und Bauelemente. 1880 gebaut, war das Gebäude früher Lager und Stall. Viele der Originaldetails wurden erhalten und mit zeitgenössischen Stücken ergänzt. Der Raum setzt sich aus drei Ebenen zusammen, die durch bewegliche Paneele und Öffnungen vertikale und horizontale Verbindungen zulassen. Küche, Esszimmer, Bibliothek und Computerraum liegen unten; Schlafzimmer und Aufnahmestudio befinden sich in den beiden oberen Etagen. Die auffälligsten Charakteristika sind das schräge Dach, eine gebogene Wand, galvanisiertes Metall, Holzpfeiler und ein sichtbares Gewirr aus Deckenbalken.

L'originalité de ce loft, conçu pour un couple musicien/producteur, réside dans l'emploi de divers matériaux et éléments de construction. Édifié en 1880, cet espace était jadis une étable/entrepôt. Nombre de caractéristiques originelles ont été préservées, des pièces d'époque étant ajoutées. L'espace, sur trois niveaux, offre des relations verticales et horizontales. Panneaux mobiles et ouvertures permettent la combinaison de certaines pièces. Cuisine, salle à manger, bibliothèque et salle informatique se situent au premier niveau, les chambres et le studio d'enregistrement occupant les niveaux supérieurs. Un plafond pentu, un mur courbe, du métal galvanisé, des piliers en bois et un enchevêtrement apparent de poutres constituent quelques points saillants de ce loft.

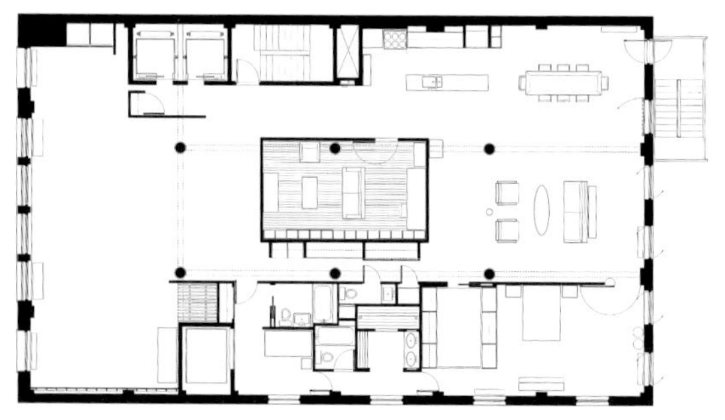

Private Residence
Tony Foy

Photos: © Dennis Krukowski
Completion date: 1996

This dwelling's originality comes from innovative architectural details and interior design. The architect worked with different horizontal and vertical levels to enhance and define the space. Walls, instead of physical barriers, are used as flexible, mobile, or even invisible elements. Other important characteristics are the decor and the interesting mixture of styles. Neutral walls act as a backdrop for colorful objects, original furniture, and radiant flowers. The frame-like windowpanes invite the resident to contemplate the views like works of art. The subtle assortment of styles and techniques in this apartment create a harmonious existence, which is perfectly suited to the cosmopolitan, urban surroundings.

Die Originalität dieser Wohnung rührt von den innovativen Architekturdetails und der Inneneinrichtung her. Der Architekt arbeitete mit verschiedenen horizontalen und vertikalen Ebenen, um den Raum zu vergrößern und zu definieren. Wände sind statt physischer Schranken flexible, bewegliche oder sogar unsichtbare Elemente. Weitere Besonderheiten sind das Dekor und der Stilmix. Neutrale Wände dienen als Hintergrund für farbenfrohe Objekte, originelle Möbel und prachtvolle Blumen. Die Fenster gleichen Bilderrahmen und laden den Bewohner ein, die Aussicht wie ein Kunstwerk zu genießen. Die subtile Auswahl der Stile und Techniken schaffen eine harmonische Existenz, die perfekt zu der kosmopoliten, urbanen Umgebung passt.

L'originalité du lieu tient aux détails architecturaux novateurs et au design intérieur. L'architecte s'est appuyé sur différents niveaux horizontaux et verticaux pour rehausser et définir l'espace. Loin d'être des obstacles physiques, les murs deviennent des éléments flexibles, mobiles voire invisibles. La décoration et un mélange de styles intéressant constituent d'autres traits remarquables. Les murs neutres offrent un arrière-plan aux objets colorés, meubles originaux et fleurs rayonnantes. Les vitres, encadrées, invitent le résident à contempler le panorama comme une œuvre d'art. L'assortiment subtil de styles et de techniques engendrent une existence harmonieuse, en accord parfait avec les alentours urbains et cosmopolites.

TINGUELY